# THE DISOBEDIENT SOCIETY

# THE DISOBEDIENT SOCIETY

## Mat Little

new-compass.net

*The Disobedient Society*
2019 © by Mat Little

ISBN 978-82-93064-55-8
ISBN 978-82-93064-16-5 (ebook)

Published by New Compass Press
Grenmarsvegen 12,
N–3912 Porsgrunn,
Norway

Design and layout by Eirik Eiglad

New Compass presents ideas on participatory democracy, social ecology, and movement building—for a free, secular, and ecological society.

new-compass.net
2019

# Contents


Introduction 7

1. Obedience to Authority in the Era of Neoliberalism 15

2. Is Obedience Natural? 63

3. The "Free" Labourer and the Eclipse of Scarcity 105

4. The Disobedient Society 145

# Introduction

History began because of disobedience. In the Biblical myth, Adam and Eve disobey God's order not to eat the forbidden fruit and, as a result, are banished from the Garden of Eden. "The act of disobedience broke the primary bond with nature and made them individuals," says Erich Fromm. "Original Sin, far from corrupting man, set him free; it was the beginning of history."[1]

1    "Disobedience as a Psychological and Moral Problem." In Erich Fromm, *On Disobedience* (HarperCollins, 2010), 2.

In Greek myth, Prometheus stole fire from the gods and gave it to humanity, thus allowing human history to start. He was chained to a rock to endure eternal torment for his crime, but refused to repent.

It might seem that the foundation myth of disobedience is still upheld today. We are living through the days of protest. Between 2011 and 2015 there were over 800 mass demonstrations in cities around the world, more than at any other time in history.[2] Societies, both in the Euro-American heartlands and the so-called developing world, are angry, discontent and enflamed with politics. The quiet, unruffled days of the "roaring nineties" seem a distant memory.

However, the turbulence is, in my opinion, deceptively superficial. Just as neoliberalism, as the guiding philosophy of the world's governments, refused to lie down and die in the aftermath of the 2008 economic crash, so its precepts of personal behaviour have proved remarkably resilient. And what neoliberalism did, in terms of the microcosm of everyday life, was to camouflage obedience. According to its leading intellectual lights, obedience was an integral part of the modus operandi of totalitarian and collectivist governments. The citizen obeyed the orders of the supreme leader or the "director" and had no ideals of their own. However, once the economy was liberated from the entanglements of governments and individuals could freely contract with each other, obedience vanished from view. Because workers (allegedly) *voluntarily* sold their labour

---

2    Guy Standing, *The Corruption of Capitalism* (Biteback Publishing, 2016), 290.

services to employers, the resulting relationship was one of equality and symmetry. They, in Ludwig Von Mises' phrase, jointly determined the course of events.

Chapter One begins with one of the most famous (or infamous) psychological experiments of all time—Stanley Milgram's obedience investigations of the early 1960s. Milgram, and many others, thought he had detected a terrible flaw in human nature—the propensity of individuals to obey the orders of superiors to carry out atrocities that they *personally* felt nothing but revulsion for. But Milgram discovered a peculiar feature of obedience—it was dependent on free will. An obedient person did not have to agree with the content of the acts they were ordered to undertake—they might be horrified by them—but they had to voluntarily agree to be obedient. Without this element of collusion, compliance could only be ensured by perpetual surveillance. Thus, to work, obedience had to be internalised, and sanctions for disobedience to come primarily from within.

Neoliberalism rests on this internalisation of obedience. Its vehemence that obedience has been annulled because of the voluntary nature of the labour contract is an ideological construction. Because the labour contract is, in essence, simply an agreement of obedience in exchange for wages. If, in reality, the person selling their labour does not do so voluntarily—if they need income to support themselves or others—they are not free to choose. However, provided this process is widely *perceived as voluntary* (the labourer is "free" in contrast to the slave, serf or totalitarian subject who obviously isn't) then the subsequent elicitation of obedience by the employer should be smooth and uncontested. Thus neoliberalism has worked unremittingly to, in Margaret Thatcher's words, "change the soul"—to place the selling of labour and the labour contract out of reach of political considerations, to reify it into an undisputed part of the world.[3]

Chapter Two starts from Milgram's attempt to explain the existence of obedience. He believed its ubiquitous presence was a sign that it had to be an evolutionary adaptation. Homo sapiens, he concluded, are innately obedient. I test this hypothesis against Murray Bookchin's contention that humanity has two natures: First nature, a strictly biological realm which dictates that we act collectively and enables us to alter the world around us, and second nature, a domain of experimentation and innovation that is not governed by the dictates of natural selection. That humanity has not evolved to be obedient does not mean obedience doesn't exert a tenacious hold. Custom, conservatism and genuflection to authority—allied to the coercive strength of the powerful— can, as history shows, prolong oppression and suffering for thousands of years and make the unendurable endure. But those forces are not invincible and not the outcome of biological laws.

Capitalism—in the guise of inescapable wage labour— is now the primary manifestation of obedience in the world. In Chapter Three, I examine the idea that, through the rise of technology, the wage system is coming to be seen as a form of unnecessary suffering—that, like chattel

---

3    "Economics are the method. The object is to change the heart and soul." Margaret Thatcher, interviewed in *The Sunday Times*, 1 May 1981.

slavery and serfdom in past centuries—it is being rendered economically superfluous. I consider the assertion that, in a consummate historical irony, capitalism will be undone not by implacable opposition but by its own competitive dynamism. Specifically, the coming of zero marginal costs— the reduction to close to nothing of the price of producing additional copies of a given product—will inexorably erode profit, destroy wage labour and sweep the ground from under the feet of the masters of the universe. I don't believe this will happen, partly because the system's dynamism is overstated by both friends and enemies but, at the same time, capitalism is losing precious legitimacy, becoming viewed as simply a method for elites to extract value, rather than an enhancement of the wealth and welfare of society. For this reason, "post-scarcity"—material abundance and sufficiency in the means of life for all people—is now a real threat to a capitalist system which depends for its very existence on the preservation of scarcity.

In the final chapter, I contemplate what a disobedient society might look like. I believe that our current representative political systems—in which consent to the wishes of the powerful is prised from a mass of people reduced to silence for the vast majority of the time—is only appropriate to a society in which free time is devoured by work and career aspirations. For a model of what arrangements could suit a society in which those preoccupations have been left behind, I look to the council democracy that Hannah Arendt regarded as the "lost treasure"[4] of the revolutionary tradition

4   Hannah Arendt, *On Revolution* (Faber & Faber, 1963; 2016), 284.

and to one contemporary manifestation of this "bottom-up" democracy—Rojava in Syria.

Arendt believed that, throughout history, freedom—a realm beyond command and obedience—was only possible because small minorities forced the vast majority of people to "bear the burden of life for them."[5] Thus, by its very nature, freedom was an exclusive commodity. Now, that realm of freedom, through an end to scarcity, can potentially be universalised. However, such a disobedient society might still be conformist—that is, while wearing the garb of pluralism and receptivity, it could exert an invisible pressure to echo the presumptions of the dominant majority. Hence, I believe Bookchin's concept of dissensus is essential. Dissensus is the cherishing of disagreement for its own sake. It entails the right, even obligation, of minorities to continue their dissent even after a decision has been reached. Without dissensus, direct democracy could quickly degenerate into conformity with a monolithic general will.

I make no pretence to originality. This book is strongly influenced by two subterranean political traditions. One is social ecology, mainly represented by the figure of Murray Bookchin. According to social ecology, obedience is a social development, a product of second nature, rather than a trait bred into the human organism. Social ecology is an attempt to closely examine the course of human history, and pre-history, to see at what points command and obedience—and more broadly hierarchy—took root and diffused. It seeks to understand the inherent logic of human development—how

---

5    Ibid., 110.

it began and unfolded, where it is now and where, potentially, it could go given its essential characteristics.

But there is another political tradition whose presence kept making itself felt during the writing of this book. That tradition is republican freedom or classical republicanism. As its name implies, this way of thinking goes back to the Romans and the Greeks and it asserts that a person is not free if subject to another's will. It does not matter if this domination comes about voluntarily or through coercion, the problem is the resulting subjection. Freedom means non-domination. Hence, republican freedom was integral to the 19th century concept of wage slavery—the idea, propagated by Karl Marx and many other non-Marxists, even non-socialists—that if workers were dependent on others—employers—for the means of life, they were not free and the wage system was, in reality, a form of slavery. We are living with a resurgent wage system now and if this book makes one solid prediction, it is that the idea of wage slavery will make a comeback as the 21st century progresses.

Hannah Arendt was also heavily influenced by classical republicanism but in a different way. Looking back to the Greek polis, she believed freedom resided in a *political* realm. This was a sphere beyond subjection and domination, one devoid of command and obedience, where people met as equals, discussed, disagreed and formed opinions. However, Arendt was implacably hostile to the idea that the political realm be sullied by the concerns of the social (broadly the economy) or the private realm (or vice versa). It was a place of government and nothing else. Marx, by contrast, looked forward to human material emancipation, a technologically advanced society that gave its inhabitants the freedom to choose the activities they wanted to engage in, but thought this would mean "the end of politics."[6] He thought of politics in negative terms, as an instrument for rule and domination. Probably, in the future, an emancipatory political movement will have to try and meld these two traditions together.

Contrary to the proclivities assumed to be an indelible part of human nature, such a movement will, in Arendt's words, assert both "a strong disinclination to obey" and an equally resolute "disinclination to dominate and command."[7]

*September 2019*

---

6   See Marco Rosaire Rossi, *A Politics for the 99%* (New Compass Press, 2014), 49-54.

7   "On Violence," in Hannah Arendt, *The Crises of the Republic* (Harcourt Brace & Company, 1969), 139.

# Chapter One

# Obedience to Authority in the Era of Neoliberalism

It took 12 years for the experimenter to try and explain his findings. Perhaps because they were so hard to explain. In the summer of 1961, 28-year-old social psychologist Stanley Milgram had demonstrated, in the serene surroundings of Yale University's campus, the willingness of ordinary people to inflict possibly lethal electric shocks on an innocent stranger. They remained undeterred even when the victim pleaded for them to stop. But there were reasons not to jump to hasty conclusions. Possibly the first subjects of the experiment—Yale undergraduates—were an unusually aggressive bunch. So Milgram turned to a more representative sample: professionals, white-collar and manual workers, the unemployed. However, the outcome was the same. The location was changed, from the elegant Yale University "interaction laboratory" to a functional office in a nearby industrial town. The propensity to exact pain was reduced, but not significantly. The original participants had all been male. Would women, thought of as more empathetic and resistant to hurting others, behave differently? Not in this setting—in female only variations of the experiment the readiness to shock the victim was almost identical. Finally, the experiment was internationalised. It was repeated in Italy, Germany, South Africa, Jordan and Australia. But, if anything, the numbers meting out the punishments were even higher.[1]

In 1973, Milgram belatedly took pen to paper. He started by rejecting the view that a psychological experiment was a unique event, bereft of lessons which could be generalised to society at large. "Any social occasion," he asserted, "has unique properties to it, and a social scientist's task is finding the principles that run through this surface diversity." But society was unable to penetrate beneath the veneer,

---

1    Thomas Blass, author of *The Man Who Shocked the World: The Life and Legacy of Stanley Milgram*, has calculated that in the Milgram Obedience experiments conducted in the US, 61% of subjects were fully obedient. In other countries, the obedience rate was 66%. Thomas Blass, "The Obedience Experiment at 50," *Association for Psychological Science, Observer Magazine*, 31 August, 2011.

upholding "a seriously distorted view of the determinants of human action"; one which renders predictions about how people will actually behave in real life hopelessly naïve. Milgram asked an educated cross-section of people (college professors, psychiatrists, students and middle-class adults) how they expected people to act in his experiment. The almost universal response was that virtually all participants would refuse to shock the victim. Only a pathological fringe—one in a thousand—would continue to the end of the dial and inflict 450-volt shocks, enough to conceivably kill the recipient. Innate human decency would come to the fore. In reality, in Milgram's basic experiment, 65% of subjects do proceed to the "end of the dial."

As is well known, Milgram's experiment was based on a deception. In truth, no-one was being shocked.[2] Depicted as a memory experiment to test the effect of punishment on a person's ability to learn, actors played the parts of the experimenter and the "victim"/learner. The draw to see who would take on the role of the "teacher" and "learner" was rigged so that the learner would always be the same 47-year-

---

2    In terms of the hazy popular recollection of the Milgram experiment, the fact that no actual shocks took place is sometimes forgotten. *Ghostbusters* (1984), one of the most enduringly popular films of the last 40 years, contains an experiment in which the rationale, "testing the effect of negative reinforcement on ESP," mimics Milgram's cover-story. With the difference that Bill Murray in Ghostbusters was actually delivering minor electric shocks.

old auditor.[3] In view of the teacher, the learner was strapped to a chair in an adjacent room and electrodes placed on his arm. The teacher was instructed to read out word pairs and if the learner incorrectly remembered any of the pairs, they were ordered to give them an electric shock—starting with 15 volts and leading up 450 volts (labelled "Danger—Severe Shock" on the machine). In reality, the learner sat, electrode-free, in the next room, pressing play on a tape recorder at various points. The recordings—which could be heard through the wall—involved cries of pain, warnings ("my heart's starting to bother me"), protests ("I refuse to go on" and "Get me out of here!") and then agonised screams. Finally, after the 330-volt mark, an ominous silence reigned.

Milgram was castigated for the unethical nature of his experiment. Participants were deceived about its true nature, they experienced great psychological and physical strain through inflicting what they believed were genuinely dangerous electric shocks, and some seem to have suffered enduring harm. However, although Milgram's experiment was deceptive, it was not a fraud. He showed that society, does indeed embrace "a seriously distorted view of the determinants of human action." The experiment has been replicated many times since the 1960s and in many different cultures, with strikingly similar results. Thomas Blass, Milgram's biographer, is convinced he "identified one of the

---

3   In the experiments Milgram oversaw the learner was always male; the same person undertook the role throughout. I know of no variations where the recipient of the "shocks'" was a woman and whether this would have had an impact on the results.

universals, or constants, of human behavior, straddling time and place."[4]

When Milgram finally came to analyse the experiment, his concern was to demonstrate the universality of misplaced ideals about human nature. Not only remote observers, but those who watched the experiment unfold through a one-way mirror, were sure the results would be very different. "Observers often expressed disbelief upon seeing a subject administer more and more powerful shocks to the victim," said Milgram. They were convinced that compassion, empathy and conscience would win out. They didn't. But he was also adamant that the opposite interpretation—what can be classed the pessimistic view—was equally erroneous. "When the experiment is first described to ordinary men and women," wrote Milgram, "they immediately think in terms of the 'beast in man coming out,' sadism, the lust for inflicting pain on others, the outpouring of the dark and evil part of the soul." In this view, the experiment merely supplied a socially acceptable pretext for these unconscious drives to be given free reign. And such an interpretation was not just the wayward hunch of the popular mind. A devotee of Sigmund Freud would look upon Milgram's experiment in precisely this light. In Freudian terms, Milgram had simply enabled the pent-up aggression harboured by all people to be released. Given permission to inflict pain on another person, the subjects merely take advantage of the temporary lifting of the threat of censure to do what they secretly want. After all, "man is a wolf to man."

---

4    Blass, "The Obedience Experiment at 50."

But while Milgram did not deny that aggression was part of human nature, he regarded this supposedly realist explanation for his findings as no more enlightening than naïve expectations. "Men [sic] do become angry; they do act hatefully and explode in rage against others," he wrote. "But not here." Two variations on his basic experiment indicate that something other than aggression was at play. In one condition subjects are given free choice about the level of shock they inflicted on the learner, and merely told it was fine if they decide to go up to the highest shock on the board. The vast majority, however, choose to remain below shocks that were audibly painful to the victim or engendered protests. In another, the experimenter unexpectedly aborts the experiment mid-way through after the learner's cries of pain become intense. The learner, however, demands to go on (it would be an insult to his "manliness" not to). The result is that all subjects go along with the experimenter's wish to halt the experiment—not a single one takes advantage of the conflict to continue administering shocks. "It is not enough to say that the situation provided a setting in which it was acceptable for the subject to hurt another person," concluded Milgram.

So, if both optimistic and pessimistic conceptions of human nature proved hopelessly inadequate to explain Milgram's experiment, what was really going on? The title of Milgram's 1974 book which belatedly analysed the experiment—*Obedience to Authority*—supplies the answer. "It is the extreme willingness of adults to go to almost any lengths on command of an authority that constitutes the chief finding of the study," the author wrote. Palpably, the volunteers did not like what they believed they were doing. Ordered to shock the victim by the experimenter, they experienced great stress—they shook, sweated and trembled. Some dug their fingernails into their flesh or laughed hysterically. But temperament was irrelevant—despite visible manifestations of strain and conflict most participants (two-thirds) went on obeying even when they had good reason to think the victim was unconscious or dead.[5]

## An Agent for the Wishes of Authority

The reason, according to Milgram, that a non-sadistic person could willingly inflict pain on another human being, was that they had entered a different "state of mind." In such a trance-like state their moral values were suspended—they no longer saw themselves as responsible for their actions, but obeyed the instructions of someone in a position of authority. Milgram termed this attitude the *agentic state* (so-called because the subject is merely an agent for the wishes of another person):

---

5   Of course, the experiment had another side. It repeatedly demonstrated that around one-third of participants did disobey and refuse to go on. And in some variations that proportion increased dramatically. Most notably, in conditions of peer rebellion (actors, posing as additional teachers, who refused to shock the victim), obedience dropped to around 10%. "The individual is weak in his solitary opposition to authority but the group is strong," Milgram concluded: "this is a lesson every revolutionary group learns."

> From a subjective standpoint, a person is in a state of agency when he defines himself in a social situation in a manner that renders him open to regulation by a person of higher status. In this condition the individual no longer views himself as responsible for his own actions but defines himself as an instrument for carrying out the wishes of others.[6]

The agentic state was, he said, the "keystone" of his analysis and the "master attitude" from which all obedient behaviour flowed. He contrasted it to the condition of *autonomy*—as when a person's acts flow naturally from their own desires or wishes. Moreover, the agentic state was not some artificially induced laboratory gimmick. Milgram believed he had isolated "an alteration of attitude" that is replicated countless times in real world situations.

> The occasion we term a psychological experiment shares its essential properties with other situations composed of subordinate and superordinate roles. In all such circumstances the person responds not so much to the content of what is required but on the basis of his relationship to person who requires it. Indeed, where the legitimate authority is the source of action, *relationship overwhelms content*. That is what is meant by the importance of social structure, and that is what is demonstrated in the present experiment.[7]

---

6  Stanley Milgram, *Obedience to Authority: An Experimental View* (Pincher & Martin, 2005), 135.

7  Ibid., 174.

However, for "relationship to overwhelm content" and for a person to allow themselves to become a mere vessel, a conduit for the wishes of others, certain conditions have to apply. In particular, the process has to be perceived as voluntary. This creates a kind of moral obligation on the part of the participant which binds them to the role they have chosen to fulfil. By voluntarily agreeing to become an agent for the wishes of another, the subject feels that they should comply with whatever instructions are given. Subjective feelings about the content of the acts they are instructed to perform are overridden.

Obedience, Milgram stressed, is not the same as coercion. The latter is dependent on some kind of material threat to enforce compliance and works only as long as surveillance is maintained. In a purely coercive situation, it does not matter what is going on in the head of the coerced individual; their actions alone count. With obedience, however, an element of collusion between the order-giver and order-taker always has to be present. In the real world, obedience and coercion are invariably interwoven, yet on some level the obedient subject has to *choose* to be obedient.

In contemporary society, said Milgram, the individual's attitude to authority is conditioned by a reward structure, which requites obedience and punishes rebellion. Reward has many guises, he claimed, but the most "ingenious" form is that of promotion. Through promotion the individual feels a "profound emotional gratification" while the continuity of the hierarchical form is perpetuated. Thus, obedience has a decidedly quotidian aspect to it. It does not manifest itself in a "dramatic confrontation of opposed wills or philosophies," said Milgram, "but is embedded in a larger atmosphere where social relationships, career aspirations and technical routines set the dominant tone."

## Obedience and the Nazis

The archetypal obedient individual, in Milgram's eyes, was thus not a feverishly aggressive person exploiting a position of power but a mere operative who has been given a job to do and strives to do it well. In *Obedience to Authority,* one flesh and blood person seems to embody this archetype. Adolf Eichmann, the Nazi bureaucrat who 12 years before had been hanged in Jerusalem for overseeing Jewish deportations to extermination camps during the Second World War, haunts its pages. In his trial, Eichmann had proclaimed his lack of guilt, legal and moral. He had been, he insisted, merely a functionary who had followed the orders of those above him in the Nazi hierarchy. This seemed to preordain Milgram's findings—Eichmann was a classic case of a person trapped inside the agentic state. Bound by an oath of allegiance and of office, Eichmann diligently carried out the instructions of the Nazi leaders, without personally sharing the same annihilationist desires ("personally" he had nothing against Jews). "I did not persecute Jews with avidity and passion. That is what the government did," he told the trial. "At that time obedience was demanded, just as in the future it will also be demanded of the subordinate."[8]

---

8   Adolf Eichmann, "In His Own Words: Eichmann's Final Plea," available at Remember.org.

Milgram was fascinated by the Eichmann trial which began a few months before his obedience experiments. He was the child of Jewish parents who had come to America from Eastern Europe during the First World War and his wider family included Holocaust survivors; one of the motivations behind the obedience experiment was somehow to explain the Holocaust. Hence, the figure of Adolf Eichmann, the "uninspired bureaucrat who simply sat at his desk and did his job," which incidentally involved sending millions to their deaths, loomed large. So close was the assumed link that a fellow psychologist, Gordon Allport, used to refer to Milgram's laboratory fabrication as "the Eichmann experiment."

In reality, however, Eichmann was a particularly poor real-world illustration of Milgram's findings. His defence that he was just following orders, an echo of the Nuremberg trials, was just that—a defence conceived to forestall the threat of execution. The truth was somewhat different. Far from being a low-level functionary, Eichmann was a convinced National Socialist who fervently believed in the righteousness of the cause he was serving. In 1957, three years before he was captured and taken to Israel, Eichmann had been interviewed by Willem Sassen, a Dutch former SS member who was part of the circle of Nazis in Argentina, where Eichmann was hiding out. In these transcripts, the image he presents is vastly different to that of the obedient subordinate reluctantly obeying his superiors. "I worked relentlessly to kindle the fire. I was not just a recipient of orders," he told Sassen. "Had I been that, I would have been an imbecile. I was an idealist."[9]

Eichmann was, in fact, consciously *disobedient* towards his superiors at times. Had he been immersed in Milgram's agentic state, as a lieutenant-colonel in the SS, he should have faithfully carried out the orders of its leader, Heinrich Himmler. In reality, towards the end of the Second World War, when Himmler ordered his subordinates to "take good care of the Jews"—out of a belief that this would secure lenient treatment from the soon-to-be victorious Allies—Eichmann, in Hannah Arendt's words, "sabotaged his orders as much as he dared."[10] Eichmann's "obedience" was not to his superiors at all but to Hitler personally, an unerring devotion known as the *Füherprinzip*.

The example of Eichmann turned out to be particularly incongruous, but, in truth, most of the real-world atrocity stories cited by Milgram or later commentators to give credence to the findings of the obedience experiment did not quite fit. There were three fundamental conditions without which the experiment might well have earned the description, "disobedience to authority." (i) Participation had to be established as a matter of free choice—the free agent condition. (ii) The subject's acts did not flow from the self—rather they became an agent for the instructions of a legitimate authority. (iii) The subject was free to disobey, or to leave, at any point. But the most famous accounts of

---

9   Alan Rosenthal, "Eichmann, Revisited," *Jerusalem Post*, 20 April 2011.

10   Hannah Arendt, *Eichmann in Jerusalem* (Penguin 2006), 145.

barbarous actions cited as illustrating the ethical dilemma illuminated by the experiment all contravene at least one of these conditions. Eichmann, for example, *may* have been morally repulsed by the human consequences of his actions but he overcame these qualms because he regarded them as necessary to advance the cause of National Socialism—that is to say, his actions did, indeed, flow from his inner core, not that of his superiors alone.[11] Atrocities carried out during the Vietnam War, such as the My Lai massacre of hundreds of unarmed civilians, including infants, in 1968, (cited by Milgram in *Obedience to Authority*) were the actions of a conscript army—participation cannot be classed as voluntary.[12] More recent crimes which Milgram's experiment has been claimed to shed light on have similar flaws. For example, the systematic torture of prisoners at Abu Ghraib prison in Baghdad during the Iraq War in 2003

---

11  Milgram claimed the obedience experiment in some way mimicked the ideological justifications behind heinous acts in the real world. Participants in the experiment believed they were advancing scientific knowledge, just as the Nazis, for example, justified the extermination of the Jews by presenting it as vital for the survival of Germany and Aryan civilisation. However, the benign "cause" being served by the experiment was remarkably flimsy when compared to the fervency of totalitarian, nationalistic or religious rationalisations. In fact, it resembles the paper-thin claims, so commonplace today, that jobs serve some ethical purpose.

12  In almost all cases of major wars, states, though they may ride a wave of voluntary enthusiasm for a while, soon resort to conscription and compel primarily young men to fight.

does indeed seem to correspond, as per Milgram, to actions ordained by the higher echelons of a hierarchy (in this case the US military) to be carried out by subordinates. But those subordinates, although not conscripts, were still subject to military discipline and not free to disobey or simply walk out. Coercion, not free choice, applied.

## The Contractual Roots of Obedience

However, once the reflex of always linking the Milgram experiment to atrocities, torture and genocide is overcome, a different type of obedience comes into view. One which is ubiquitous, even mundane, but nonetheless conforms to the three overriding conditions of the experiment—the perception of voluntary entry, the performance of actions unrelated to personal desires that originate with "authority figures," and the freedom to end the arrangement at any point. That type of obedience is the labour contract.

The Milgram experiment has become famous for showing how the inner compulsion to obey authority is so strong that for many people it overcomes the abhorrence they feel for personally inflicting pain on other people. However, Milgram also conducted 19 variations on his classic experiment. One of these demonstrates how obedience becomes nearly universal once it is detached from personal responsibility for horrific acts. In this variation, subjects were asked to arrange the word-pair tests for the putative learning experiment, while an actor actually pushed the trigger, "shocking" the victim. Entrusted with an administrative, though nonetheless essential, role, 37 out of 40 adults allowed the experiment to continue until the highest possible shock. This figure—92.5%—was the highest obedience rate recorded out of all of the experimental variations Milgram undertook. Subsequent, "Milgramesque" experiments have demonstrated the resonance of the employment role for participants. In 2008, Professor Jerry Burger of Santa Clara University in California replicated Milgram's experiment, with certain ethical adjustments. Several of the subjects who "shocked" the victim up to the permitted 150-volt level, defended their actions by saying that they were just doing their job.[13]

Such justifications are to be expected. For society gives its blessing to voluntary obedience; regarding it as essential to the coordination of large numbers of people in complex economic endeavours. Under the ideology of our times, for a person not be obedient, even enthusiastically so, after they have contractually agreed to perform a certain role is not a sign of a healthy independence of mind, but rather of pathology. For Milgram obedience was humanity's "fatal flaw," the submersion of a person's "unique personality" into institutional anonymity, the sacrifice of precious autonomy for the irresponsible cocoon of the agentic state. However,

---

13  See ABC Television Channel's Milgram Experiment remake (available at youtube.com/watch?v=JnYUl6wlBF4). The ethical adjustments were that subjects were instructed to shock only up to the 150-volt mark (compared to 450 volts in the original experiment), that they were told in advance that the experiment might involve deception and they were pre-screened by a clinical psychologist.

Milgram was writing in the 1970s. The neoliberal ideology that has grown so dominant since then views obedience in quite a different light. If voluntarily undertaken—as in a labour contract—obedience should morally follow. Far from a fatal flaw, obedience becomes a mark of freedom; a sign that we somehow collaboratively construct the economy from the bottom-up, through thousands of freely undertaken contracts.

## Obedience and the Pioneers of Neoliberalism

This attitude was most striking in the thought of the Austrian free market economist, Ludwig Von Mises. A pioneer of neoliberalism, Von Mises was a founder of the Mont Pelerin Society, the élite intellectual network formed in 1947 that sought—extraordinarily successfully—to win the "battle of ideas" against Keynesianism and in favour of classical liberal economics. He was a major influence on subsequent "libertarians" such as Ayn Rand. Von Mises maintained there were two very different kinds of social cooperation—one based on contract and coordination and the other marked by command and subordination. He termed the latter hegemony and thought it embodied in irredeemably coercive structures like chattel slavery, serfdom and Stalinist communism. Cooperation stemming from voluntarily undertaken contracts—the definitive example being the labour contract whereby a person rents themselves out and agrees to act under another's instructions—was, by contrast, an utterly different beast:

> Where and as far as cooperation is based on contract, the logical relation between the cooperating individuals is symmetrical. They are all parties to interpersonal exchange contracts. John has the same relation to Tom as Tom has to John. Where and as far as cooperation is based on command and subordination, there is the man who commands and there are those who obey his orders. The logical relation between these two classes of men is asymmetrical. There is a director and there are people under his care. The director alone chooses and directs; the others—the wards—are mere pawns in his actions.[14]

According to Von Mises, what distinguishes the contractual bond from the hegemonic bond is the freedom of the individual to "determine the course of events."[15] If individuals contract with each other they merely exchange definite quantities of goods or services. Under a hegemonic societal body, however, only the director is "free to choose." Subordinates "no longer act for themselves" but "have one freedom only: to obey without asking questions." The worker becomes "subject to the discretionary power of his superiors." It makes no difference, claimed Von Mises, whether the director—the order giver—is paternalistic or despotic. All that counts is the nature of the system.

Eleven years before the Milgram experiment and a quarter of a century before *Obedience to Authority*, Von Mises was making a classic statement about the nature of obedience.

---

14  Ludwig Von Mises, *Human Action: A Treatise on Economics* (Martino Publishing, 2012), 196.

15  Ibid., 197.

Milgram claimed that in transitioning from autonomy to a system of hierarchical control, individuals undergo a profound attitudinal shift which he termed "the agentic state"; they are transformed into an agent for the wishes of another. Von Mises saw individuals trapped inside the "hegemonic bond" as mere pawns in the hands of superiors. Milgram classified the protagonists as "subordinates" and "superordinates." Von Mises called them "wards" and "directors." And while Milgram saw this social order as internalised within the individual, thus ensuring its perpetuation, Von Mises was adamant that in obeying time after time, the subaltern "contributes his share to the continuous existence of the hegemonic societal body."[16]

However, for Von Mises, the classical liberal, obedience was a characteristic of only some kinds of social structures. Serfdom, slavery, communism and even the welfare state (*Wohlfahrtsstaat*) were all guilty of paternalism—oppressive or benevolent—which resulted in a plethora of directives and regulations, all formulated at the instigation of those at the summit of the hierarchy. Once, however, the labourer becomes "free," obedience simply vanishes. Then the worker merely sells his services on the market as a commodity like any other. The employer, in their turn, purchases these services at market price. Just as both parties voluntarily

---

16  Ibid. Von Mises was making a basically existential point that
     a person ultimately chooses whether to submit to hegemonic
     control. However, this was, in his view, utterly different from a
     person voluntarily choosing to exchange goods or services with
     another "free" individual.

embark on the relationship, both are free to end it at any point. Equality and symmetry reign. "John has the same relation to Tom as Tom has to John."

Von Mises, in other words, erases obedience exactly where Milgram finds it. For Milgram the free will of the participant is a crucial condition of ensuing compliance. It creates a sense of obligation which binds the subject to their role. The other indispensable feature of the Milgram experiment was that subjects had to be free to sever the relationship if their conscience dictated they could not go on. Under these parameters, approximately two-thirds of Milgram's participants prove willing to obey—to act in ways utterly contrary to their personal desires and voluntarily become an agent in a system of hierarchical control. Von Mises, by contrast, sees nothing amiss in a person temporarily becoming an agent for the wishes of another, provided they are not coerced into it and are free to leave. Indeed, it is the hallmark of a free society. "Human civilisation as it has been hitherto known to historical experience," he contended "is preponderantly a product of contractual [i.e. voluntary] relations."[17]

To Friedrich Hayek, Von Mises' contemporary and intellectual soulmate, the mortal danger was "collectivism," a shapeshifting threat that encompassed not merely totalitarian regimes like Nazi Germany and Stalinist Russia, but the "socialist" governments of the post-Second World War era in Europe. The latter were equally menacing because, to Hayek, the practice of socialism, or economic planning, was

---

17  Ibid., 198.

always totalitarian. Inherent in collectivism was the very essence of obedience to authority that Milgram "discovered" in a laboratory in New England in 1961. A person in such a society had to "be prepared to actively break every moral rule he has ever known if this seems necessary to achieve to the end set for him." They had to be "completely unprincipled" and have "no ideals of their own which they want to realise." In collectivist ethics, said Hayek, expediency was the supreme rule. "There can be no limit to what its [a collectivist society's] citizens must not be prepared to do, no act which his conscience must prevent him from committing, if it is necessary for an end which the community has set itself or which his superiors order him to achieve."[18]

The antithesis of collectivism, to Hayek, was a society which cherished the "freedom of the individual." However, in keeping with the economic liberalism to which he subscribed, this individuality could only be guaranteed by competition and private property, which brought about the "effective coordination of individual efforts."[19] Significantly, competition merely *coordinated* the desires and strivings of individuals, it did not direct them. Command and obedience

---

18  Ibid., 151.

19  Ibid., 38. Private property means that the means of production are either directly owned by individuals (as in privately owned companies) or indirectly by shareholders (as in publicly floated corporations). *Private* property is not synonymous with *personal* property: possessions such as clothes, homes or bicycles. A political movement can be against private property but have no wish to interfere with personal property.

were the lynchpins of the oppressive structures of the past—chattel slavery and feudalism. They had been vanquished by 19th century liberalism, only to be resurrected by genocidal 20th century dictators and superficially benign economic planners—hence, Hayek's siren warnings about the "road to serfdom."

Doubtless Hayek's old age was leavened by the realisation that the classical liberalism he so revered was rising again—in the form of neoliberalism. And, with the triumph of neoliberalism, Hayek's and Von Mises' annulling of obedience in favour of the voluntary "coordination of individual efforts" in a competitive economy has become deeply ingrained in society. The same intransigence and unwillingness to see the reality behind the "free" labour market is evident in the pronouncements of fellow economic liberal Milton Friedman. Though a generation younger, he, like Von Mises and Hayek, was a founder member of the Mont Pelerin Society. We are in many ways living in Friedman's world. The abolition of exchange controls on capital and currency speculation, banking deregulation, the administration of basic public services by for profit organisations, swingeing cuts to corporate and high earner income tax, preference for private over public monopolies and the elimination of interventions in the market like rent controls were all advocated in Friedman's hugely influential 1962 book, *Capitalism and Freedom*. In counselling an expansive monetary policy to head off economic depression, Friedman can even be seen as prefiguring the policy of Quantitative Easing that the world's central banks took to with such abandon after the 2008 crash; a policy which has, coincidentally, markedly increased the wealth of those with share and property portfolios. But when it came to imagining the economy, Friedman thought everything ultimately came down to individuals freely contracting with each other:

> The possibility of coordination through voluntary co-operation rests on the elementary—yet frequently denied—proposition that both parties to an economic transaction benefit from it, *provided the transaction is bi-laterally voluntary and informed.*

> … Since the household always has the alternative of producing for itself, it need not enter into any exchange unless it benefits from it. Hence, no exchange will take place unless both parties do benefit from it. Co-operation is thereby achieved without coercion.

> So in the complex enterprise and money-exchange economy, cooperation is strictly individual and voluntary *provided*: (a) that enterprises are private, so that the ultimate contracting parties are individuals and (b) that individuals are effectively free to enter or not enter into any particular exchange, so that every transaction is strictly voluntary.[20]

The problem that so agitated Milgram—that of ethical individuals who allow themselves to become the amoral instruments of malevolent institutions—is simply bypassed by Friedman. The challenge for believers in liberty, he says, is to reconcile the "widespread interdependence in the economy

---

20  Milton Friedman, *Capitalism and Freedom* (University of Chicago, 2002), 13.

with individual freedom." But it turns out this reconciliation is not overly challenging. It is swiftly accomplished by the blanket assumption that all economic transactions, absent those ordained by the state, are voluntary. We are all autonomous agents, rationally deciding where our interest lies. Provided a person can choose among different employers who to rent themselves to, provided they are free to walk out if they turn out not to like what they have agreed to (one of Milgram's conditions), and provided they always have the theoretical alternative of producing the means of life themselves, there is nothing to fret about. "Co-operation," Friedman contentedly concludes "is thereby achieved without coercion."[21]

---

21  Former British Prime Minister Margaret Thatcher's famous assertion that "there is no such thing as society. There are only individual men and women. And there are families," could have been lifted straight out of Friedman and is a classic statement of the mind-set of neoliberalism. It has mostly been taken as a denial of any notion of mutualism and the obligation of benevolent social or state institutions to help people (dovetailing nicely with another claim of 1980s neoliberalism that all public servants were merely out for themselves). But there was another meaning. There was no discrepancy, Thatcher was saying, between individual desires and the corporations that employed them; the firms that sought monopoly power, maximised profit or advertised to individuals as consumers. In a free market economy, she was maintaining, it was futile to complain about what the economy does because ultimately it simply reflects your own desires. The only actors in the economy are individuals and their families. In other words, there is no such thing as the agentic state.

## Obedience and Wage Slavery

Of course, if in spite of these attendant conditions such co-operation is *not* freely given, if the economic transaction between employer and employee is *not* voluntary, then the problem of obedience and coercion remains, and the contracting individual does not, as Von Mises put it, "determine the course of events." In the 19th century, in the midst of the Industrial Revolution, much of the Left embraced the concept of wage slavery—the idea that because of deep material dependence on employers, the wage labourer was, in reality, no better off than the chattel slave. Albert Parsons, the American anarchist hanged for conspiracy in the Haymarket affair of 1886, told his trial, "The chattel slave of the past—the wage slave of today, what is the difference? Formerly the master selected the slave; today the slave selects his master and he has got to find one or else he is carried down here to my friend, the jailer."

Attitudes questioning whether "free labour" was, in truth, a genuine advance on chattel slavery were by no means confined to the Marxist or socialist Left. The American economist Henry George pursued a political philosophy quite distinct from Marxism or the socialist thought of his time. He believed that private ownership of land allowed a tiny minority of individuals to monopolise all the gains of social and technological progress through the imposition of rent and advocated a land value tax to redress the inequality stemming from the ownership of land. But in his 1879 book, *Progress and Poverty*, he was as vociferous as any leftist in his condemnation of the "enslavement of labor."

"In acknowledging the right of some individuals to exclusive use and enjoyment of the earth, we condemn others to slavery as fully and as completely as though we had formally made them chattels,"[22] proclaimed George. This was slavery "under the forms of freedom." Indeed, "our boasted freedom necessarily involves slavery," he rebuked, "so long as we recognise private property in land."[23]

So influential was the concept of wage slavery, that Abraham Lincoln, the American President credited with abolishing chattel slavery in the American Civil War, was forced to defend the institution of wage labour, not on the grounds that it was an example of voluntary cooperation, but because it was only temporary. He claimed that the "free hired laborer" was not "fixed to that condition for life" but, if they were prudent [and white and male], could save "a surplus to buy tools or land"[24] and become self-employed. This was an admission that the "free labourer" was not free at all but mired in a state of subjection.

---

22  Henry George, *Progress and Poverty* (Robert Schalkenbach Foundation, 1956), 348.

23  Ibid., 353, 357.

24  See Christopher Lasch, *The Revolt of the Elites* (W.W. Norton & Company, 1995), 67-68. According to Lasch, Lincoln "did not quarrel with his opponents' [proslavery apologists from the South] disparaging view of wage labor." Rather, he looked upon wage labour in the North as a "temporary condition leading to proprietorship". Lincoln addressed the issue in a speech in Wisconsin in 1859 and in a message to Congress, stating the thinking behind the Union cause, in 1861.

Lincoln's escape route has vanished from view but the concept of the free labourer is as illusory as it always was. The labour contract, if taken in isolation, certainly *appears* to be the epitome of equality and symmetry—the voluntary exchange of goods (money) and services (work) between two free individuals, no difference in essence from buying (or selling) a pair of shoes on Ebay and devoid of any connotations of obedience and hierarchical control. It was Karl Marx in *Capital* who described the sale and purchase of labour power as:

> a very Eden of the innate rights of man. There alone rule Freedom, Equality, Property and Bentham. Freedom, because both buyer and seller of a commodity, say of labour-power, are constrained only by their own free will. They contract as free agents, and the agreement they come to, is but the form in which they give legal expression to their common will. Equality, because each enters into relation with the other, as with a simple owner of commodities, and they exchange equivalent for equivalent. Property, because each disposes only of what is his own. And Bentham because each looks only to himself.[25]

However, Marx went on, once the contract has been inked, a very different picture emerges:

> On leaving this sphere of simple circulation or of exchange of commodities ... He, who before was the money-owner, now

---

25   Karl Marx, *Capital* (Oxford World Classics edition, 1999), 113.

strides in front as capitalist; the possessor of labour-power follows as his labourer. The one with an air of importance, smirking, intent on business; the other, timid and holding back, like one who is bringing his own hide to market and has nothing to expect but—a hiding.[26]

What appears on the surface to be voluntary and perfectly symmetrical is coercive to its core. The only reason people volunteer to exchange services for money with the owners of capital is because they lack capital in the first place. They need to feed themselves and their families, pay the rent or care for sick relatives. The exchange is, by definition, asymmetrical. And this germinal inequality leads inexorably, as in Von Mises' hegemonic bond, to workers being subject to the discretionary power of their superiors and obeying without asking questions. This holds despite the fact that employees in a market economy are unquestionably free to choose, or "free agents" as Marx put it.

According to a sociologist who embedded himself at several branches of a major UK supermarket in 2016, a toxic combination of low wages, flexible hours controlled by managers, and a weak trade union presence "at times bordered on coercion," with workers being warned, "there are plenty of people out there who need jobs." Many employees, the study observed, "felt they had no choice but to work when ordered" despite a detrimental effect on physical and mental

---

26  Ibid., 114.

health.[27] In 2017, an analysis by sociologists from Cambridge and Oxford universities found that 4.6 million people in the UK regularly experience "precarious scheduling," a practice which is endemic in the retail and care sectors. This precarity fosters a "degrading relationship with managers," the analysis concluded, with workers having to beg for schedule changes to accommodate commitments such as childcare.[28]

In the United States, the power of the employer is likely to be greater still because the default employment contract is "employment at will," which means employees can be fired for any reason or none.[29] At-will-employment, according to

---

27  Alex J. Wood, "Flexible Scheduling, degradation of Job Quality and Barriers to Collective Voice," *Human Relations*, 69:10 (2016), 1989-2010.

28  Alex J. Wood, "Powerful Times: Flexible Discipline and Schedule Gifts at Work," *Work, Employment and Society*, 32:6 (2018), 1061-1077.

29  In the UK, "employment at will" exists for the first two years of an employment contract, then rules over unfair dismissal apply. The qualifying period was one year but it was increased to two by the Conservative-Lib Dem coalition in 2012. A 2011 report for the UK government by venture capitalist Adrian Beecroft advocated the replacement of unfair dismissal with "no fault dismissal" (i.e. "employment at will") as the default employment contract but it was not taken up by ministers. However, the 5.4 million private renters in the UK (up from 2.3 million in 2001) are subject to "eviction at will": Section 21 notices by landlords permit the eviction of tenants from their homes for any reason or none. They are used extensively and are a major cause of homelessness.

Elizabeth Anderson, author of *Private Government*, "grants the employer sweeping legal authority not only over workers' lives at work but also over their off-duty conduct. Under the employment-at-will baseline, workers, in effect cede *all* of their rights to employers, except those specifically guaranteed to them by law, for the duration of the employment relationship."[30]

Apart from the power to fire workers, employers possess a wide array of sanctions to choose from. "They can and often do," says Anderson, "demote employees; cut their pay; assign them inconvenient hours or too many or too few hours; assign them more dangerous, dirty, menial or gruelling tasks; increase their pace of work; set them to fail; and, within very broad limits, humiliate or harass them."[31] The depiction of the employment contract as the outcome of voluntary negotiation between worker and employer is a convenient fiction of political theory, argues Anderson, applying only to a miniscule fraction of privileged workers at the top of society. "In purchasing command over labour," she says "employers purchase command over people."[32]

The full picture of employer authority is bound to remain largely occluded because this remains a "private" world, illuminated only by the occasional searchlight of an undercover investigation or a rare official report. The

---

30  Elizabeth S. Anderson, *Private Government: How Employers Rule Our Lives (and we don't like to talk about it)* (Princeton University Press, 2017), 53-54.

31  Ibid., 55.

32  Ibid., 57, 71.

Cambridge University researchers, quoted above, warn that zero hour contracts are merely the "tip of the iceberg" of damaging shift work. Anderson laments that aggregate statistics on labour abuse are hard to come by. We do know, for example, that fear of missing work at the Derbyshire warehouse of UK retailer Sports Direct, led to an employee giving birth in the toilets; that Sports Direct, in common with Walmart in the US, penalises "excessive chatting"; that Amazon in Scotland disciplines staff who legitimately take time off sick or that Apple inspects the personal belongings of its retail staff who are forced to wait in line to be searched for half an hour each day entirely at their own cost.[33] However, these practices have been exposed largely because they occur at the warehouses of well-known brands. What happens in the twilight world of the less familiar parts of the economy remains almost completely hidden from view. According to Anderson, investigations shining a light at the bottom of the US wage labour system have uncovered abuses, affecting mainly immigrant workers, including, "fraud, being forced to work without pay, rape and sexual harassment, beatings, torture, confinement to the workplace and to squalid housing conditions for which extortionate rent is charged, exhausting hours, isolation,

---

33  "Amazon penalises staff for taking sick days, investigation finds," *People Management*, 12 December 2016.  One case involved an employee who was hospitalized because of a kidney infection. According to a quoted lawyer, absence policies are generally becoming stricter and Amazon's approach doesn't "seem particularly unusual."

religious compulsion, and psychological manipulation and intimidation."[34] Sectors of the economy implicated in these practices include hotels, sales, agriculture, manufacturing, restaurants, health and care, construction and domestic service.

However, whenever academics deign to examine the nature of the labour contract—which is not often—it is seen, as in the classical liberal ethos of Von Mises and Friedman, as the almost pure outcome of voluntary negotiation between equals. Reflecting on "economic organization," Armen Alchian and Harold Demsetz assert that to use the language of "managing, directing or assigning workers" is "deceptive." "Telling an employee to type this letter rather than to file that document," they maintain, "is like telling a grocer to sell me this brand of tuna rather than that brand of bread."[35] Employer and employee, they insist, are continually involved in a renegotiation of contracts which must always be acceptable to both parties: "Neither the employee nor the employer is bound by any contractual obligation to continue the relationship."[36] That this utopian symmetrical exchange is confined to economics textbooks—or perhaps to the highest echelons of the labour market where individual market value is such that constant renegotiation is a possibility—is glaringly apparent. Most of us have the metaphorical gun of pressing material need pointed at our heads.

---

34  Anderson, *Private Government*, 137.

35  Ibid., 54. The paper referred to is from 1972.

36  Ibid., 55.

## Internalised Obedience

But, to neoliberalism, this flagrant discrepancy between theory and reality is far from damning; in fact it verges on irrelevant. It is not important that the labour contract is not, in reality, the arena of voluntary negotiation between equals; only that it is *perceived* as such—because with the perception of voluntary exchange, the extraction of subsequent obedience becomes a smooth and uncontested process. Milgram's agentic state, the psychological shift by which a person willingly becomes an agent for the wishes of another, is achieved effortlessly. According to Milgram, "the psychological consequence of voluntary entry is that it creates a sense of commitment and obligation which will subsequently play a part in binding the subject to his role." Obedience becomes *internalised* and the principal sanctions for disobedience come from within the person; they don't have to be imposed from outside.

However, for this process of inner obedience to take hold, the authority figure has to be seen as legitimate. Among Milgram's experimental variations were ones in which an ordinary person is substituted for the lab-coated experimenter. The result was that levels of obedience dropped sharply. Some subjects even took physical action against the unauthorised interloper when he tried, following a pre-arranged script, to administer the shocks himself. "Orders originating outside of authority lose all force," said Milgram. "It is not what subjects do but for whom they are doing it that counts." In this can be seen the crucial psychological difference between the labour contract—where an employee agrees to obey the instructions of "legitimate" authority, the employer—and a simple economic transaction, selling a car, for instance, to another person. The former rests on a posture of internally-conditioned obedience, while the latter is defined, as in the classical liberal utopia, by equality and symmetry between the participants.

Thus, the pre-eminent battle for any system of control—often more important than the actual conditions of coercion that may be enforced—is to achieve legitimacy. For if legitimacy is attained, those who rebel against the demands of authority don't merely have to organise subordinates to improve their "lot," they also have to continually fight against the notion that those demands are imbued with an unshakeable moral validity, or simply that a system of command and obedience is inevitable. The decisive struggle is within the minds of the oppressed.

That obedience today is as robustly healthy as it ever was, but successfully internalised so that it doesn't appear to exist, can be observed from the fact that the wage labour system actually functions. The vast majority of workers don't in fact continually renegotiate their contracts with their employers in a way they find pleasing. If this fantasy version of capitalism actually existed the entire system would grind to a halt. On the contrary, most employees habitually go beyond what is stipulated in their employment contract. Working to rule—strictly following designated tasks—amounts to a form of "semi strike."[37] It is known in Italy as "sciopero bianco" or

---

37  See Ha-Joon Chang, 23 *Things They Don't Tell You About Capitalism* (Allen Lane, 2010), 46-47.

"white strike," and is recognised to drastically slow down the work process, decreasing output by 30 to 50%. Thus the labour contract contains within it ingrained forms of behaviour that do not apply to the simple exchange of economic commodities. As pointed out by the great economic historian Karl Polanyi, over 70 years ago, if their labour was a simple commodity, like sugar or oil, workers should logically refuse to sell their "service" below the highest price that the buyer (the employer) was still prepared to pay:

> Consistently followed up, this means that the chief obligation of labor is to be almost continually on strike. The proposition could not be outbidden for sheer absurdity, yet it is the only logical inference from the commodity theory of labor. The source of the incongruity of theory and practice is, of course, that labor is not really a commodity and that if labor was withheld in order to ascertain its exact price (just as an increase in supply of all other commodities is withheld in similar circumstances) society would very soon dissolve for lack of sustenance.[38]

If, as Polanyi affirms, labour "is not really a commodity" (he thought that for something to be a commodity it had to be produced for sale—people, i.e. labour, and nature are not), the entire neoliberal schema of holding that all contracts—including the labour contract—should not be interfered with if they are "freely" undertaken, is revealed to be built on sand. However, to admit that would be to concede the falsity

---

38  Karl Polanyi, *The Great Transformation* (Beacon Press, 2001), 239.

of the voluntary character of the labour contract. And that contention has proved so very useful in entrenching Milgram's agentic state—the willingness to obey the instructions of legitimate authority.

Unquestionably, bare coercion has played an important role. The last time there was any spark of industrial militancy—the 1970s—the response of neoliberals was to employ the power of the state to snuff out trade union resistance. Initially the charge was that unions coerced people against their will through compelling them to become union members as a condition of employment (the closed shop). In championing "the right to work" and automatic ballots on industrial action, neoliberals could plausibly maintain they were simply upholding the threatened prerogative of voluntary economic contracts. But since then the mask has firmly slipped, revealing the underlying animus towards labour organising in principle. The hostility to trade unions per se—no matter how enthusiastically workers choose to be members or support industrial action—is palpable and unrelenting.

However, neoliberals have also worked tirelessly to "change the soul." A neoliberal meritocratic worldview has successfully redirected attention away from any notion of an oppositional relationship between employer and employee towards an immersive focus on careers and success. Characteristics such as flexibility, the ability to network, an entrepreneurial attitude and a perpetual focus on tangible results are instilled by business, the media and educational institutions. They are regarded as indispensable despite, or perhaps because, conditions of working life are visibly worsening—the rise of part-time work, freelancing and sub-contracting has meant that previously guaranteed fixtures of the working environment such as pensions, holiday and sick pay and predictable hours have vanished for many. According to Belgian psychoanalyst Paul Verhaeghe, it is no accident that all of today's "'right' characteristics"—especially competiveness and social skills—coincide with professional identity.[39] The underbelly of such a society is the prevalence of feelings of shame among people who feel they cannot live up to this inescapable "success narrative." Mental illnesses such as anxiety and depression are rife. And, notwithstanding a distinctly malleable desire for ethical careers, Milgram's agentic state—temporarily becoming an agent for legitimate authority—is assumed to be a natural part of the landscape. Milgram always claimed that the process of obedience did not involve the "dramatic confrontation of opposed wills" but was camouflaged inside career aspirations and technical routines. In the present time, this quotidian mask is fastened ever more tightly. To object to such a basic social function is not simply wrong. It is deviant, probably a sign that the dissenter is suffering from some kind of mental disorder.

"No society can be stable unless there is a basic core of value judgments that are unthinkingly accepted by the great bulk of its members," said Friedman.[40] In this way, neoliberalism is

---

39  Paul Verhaeghe, *What About Me? The Struggle for Identity in a Market-Based Society* (Scribe, 2014), 201.

40  Milton Friedman, *Capitalism and Freedom* (University of Chicago Press, 1962), 167.

revealed to be, first and foremost, an ideological project. It has not, despite its avowed promises, raised the rate of economic growth or productivity levels, brought about an increase in social wealth and real wages, re-invigorated anaemic business investment or, indeed, re-instituted a mythical free market unencumbered by the influence of the state. As a form of capitalism, it is peculiarly unsuccessful. But in one respect neoliberalism is an undoubted success story—in instilling the notion that obedience should morally follow from the wage labour relationship and that capitalism is the only conceivable game in town. "Ideological abrogation" to authority was the cognitive basis of obedience, affirmed Milgram. "Control the manner in which a man [sic] interprets his world, and you have gone a long way toward controlling his behavior."

## Forced to be Free

Our interpretation of the world has been controlled by the conviction, assiduously disseminated by classical liberalism, that a chasm exists between past and present. That true obedience is extracted by the crack of the whip, and resides solely in the coercive arrangements of previous epochs—serfdom or chattel slavery. Or in the totalitarian regimes of Nazism and Communism and even the socialistic governments of post second world war social democracy. In the present era, notwithstanding the resilience of political repression, we have entered a different age. Coercion has been replaced by a vast constellation of numberless consensual contracts, of which wage labour constitutes the major element. The employee is thus "free" in a way the serf or slave of the past palpably was not. Hayek defined freedom as "freedom from coercion, freedom from the arbitrary power of other men, release from the ties which left the individual no choice but obedience to the orders of a superior to whom he was attached."[41] If such a thing as obedience still exists—and Milgram subversively demonstrated its potency—it is confined to complying with the demands of the military or the political authorities. The economy—provided it is allowed to be free—merely coordinates immeasurable individual desires.

However, the liberation which classical liberals insist has occurred rests primarily on the fact that subordination and ownership is now only temporary and is lifted at the end of each working day. The revolution is skin deep. According to the anthropologist David Graeber wage labour is, in reality, a transformation of chattel slavery—not as conventionally assumed its mirror opposite. The earliest wage labour contracts, he asserts, were about the renting out of slaves—the slaves received a daily allocation for food, while the slave-

---

41　Friedrich Hayek, *The Road to Serfdom* (Routledge, 1944), 26. It would be hard to find a more intractable espousal of the cause of freedom but Hayek preferred "liberal dictatorship" to "democratic government devoid of liberalism," wanted to destroy trade unions and regarded encroachments on freedom of contract between employer and employee as the "road to serfdom." Fellow classical liberal, Von Mises, regarded trade unionism as a form of terrorism and thought the merit of Italian Fascism—won through saving European civilisation from the workers' movement—would "live on eternally in history."

owner was paid for the use of his "property." In slave societies such as Ancient Athens, permanent employees, including public servants, were invariably slaves. Wage labour was looked down upon as tantamount to slavery. Only much more recently have the two been regarded as diametrically opposed.

Both wage labour and slavery, says Graeber, revolve around the power to command what Marx termed "abstract labour," that is to say "what one buys when one buys a slave is the sheer capacity to work, which is also what an employer acquires when he hires a laborer." Societies dominated by wage labour are also invariably accompanied by a vehement doctrine of personal liberty but one that applies only *outside of the workplace*. Inside its confines, the relationship of command and obedience remains intact, and what goes on there either has to be idealised out of all recognition or ignored. To Graeber these militant paeans to liberty are not a sign that obedience has been extirpated but merely that it has taken another form:

> We are dealing with the same terms, differently arranged: so that rather than one class of people being able to imagine themselves as absolutely "free" because others are absolutely unfree, we have the same individuals moving back and forth the between these two positions over the course of the week and working day … so, in effect, a transfer effected just once, by sale, under a regime of slavery is transformed under capitalism into one repeated over and over again.[42]

---

42  David Graeber, *Possibilities: Essays on Hierarchy, Rebellion and Desire* (AK Press, 2007), 106.

This is not to equate, for example, the horrors of the 17th and 18th century Trans-Atlantic slave trade with wage labour. Being kidnapped, transported over the ocean in chains, working unpaid for 14 hours a day, whipped if you slack and spending your (probably short) life as the "property" of another is not the same as working for a wage. However, neither is it its antithesis. "Instead of being sold against our will into indefinite servitude, we rent ourselves out for a fee, for defined purposes and set periods of time," says film-maker Raoul Martinez. "That money is paid does not change the fact that at the heart of this arrangement is a relationship of control."[43]

Neoliberalism is the latest incarnation of Graeber's ideologies of freedom—forms of thought that eulogise liberty as a way of hiding the fact that it is conspicuously partial or applies only to some and not others.[44] In the 20 years between 1980 and 2000, the number of wage labourers in the world doubled, to nearly 3 billion; a period marked, coincidentally, by the ascendancy of neoliberalism and its insistence that the "freedom to choose" could only be realised through the competitive market. Wage labour was not merely something to be endured as a way of gaining the resources to choose in the marketplace—in mainstream economics labour is the burden for which consumption enabled by wages is the compensation—but became a moral obligation in itself. In this way, the subordination it entails could be brushed over.

"Welfare reform" in the Anglo-Saxon stomping grounds of neoliberalism became the emblem of parties of the Right

---

43  Raoul Martinez, *Creating Freedom* (Canongate Books, 2017), 93.

44  Graeber, *Possibilities*, 105.

and Centre-Left. The 1996 Welfare Reform Act (technically "The Personal Responsibility and Work Opportunity Reconciliation Act") in the United States, for instance, ended the federal guarantee of assistance to claimants, placed a two-year limit on how long benefits could be received and required recipients to spend up to 40 hours a week looking for work. According to one aide to President Bill Clinton who signed the legislation into law, "The real Clinton legacy on the poor comes down to the one word: work."[45] In the UK, around 300,000 benefit sanctions, which involve the withdrawal of income from social security claimants for anything between four weeks and three years, were imposed in 2016, for offences ranging from missing appointments with job coaches to not taking part in "mandatory work activity" or failing to apply for a job.[46] Since 2008 a "Work Capability Assessment," which assesses job readiness on the basis of abstract tasks such as reaching above your head (abstract labour—the capacity to do undefined work), has been mandatory for claimants of disability or illness benefit in Britain. Two-thirds of appeals against a decision that a claimant is "fit to work" are successful, and even if a claimant is deemed "unfit for work" many are still required to look for employment and make themselves appealing to potential employers, with sanctions at the ready if they do

---

45  Quoted in Thomas Frank, *Listen Liberal* (Scribe 2016), 115. Since the Act's introduction the number of people in the US living on $2 a day or less has more than doubled.

46  "DWP accused of misleading the public on benefit sanction numbers," *Welfare Weekly*, 25 February 2017.

not do so satisfactorily. Under "Universal Credit"—the new system of social security payments in the UK which replaces all existing benefits and is gradually being introduced across the country—the sanctions regime will be extended to people in work. Those who currently receive tax credits or housing benefit will be sanctioned if they are fired for misconduct, leave a job voluntarily or lose pay through misconduct. But while employees are to be the subject of constant monitoring and pressure, employers are reassured that Universal Credit will enable them to "access a more flexible and responsive workforce."[47]

In both the US and UK, the justification for these policies was that they would save precious public funds—it was Bill Clinton who began the mania for balanced government budgets which went viral after 2008. However, numerous studies have shown that these "entitlement" denying ordinances actually cost more money than they save.[48] They

47  See the UK Department for Work and Pensions, "Universal Credit for Employers: How it helps your business," available at gov.uk/guidances. According to one benefits analyst, Universal Credit could mean workers, fearing sanctions, "will be afraid to lose or leave a job, or even complain, no matter how badly they are treated." Ian Sinclair, "Universal Credit: Internationally unique in its harshness, and headed for 7 million of us," *Open Democracy UK*, 1 November 2017.

48  See, for example, Peter Muennig, Rishi Caleyachetty, Zohn Rosen and Andrew Korotzer, "More Money: Fewer Lives: The Cost Effectiveness of Welfare Reform in the United States," *American Journal of Public Health*, 105: 2 (2015), 324-328; Martha Gill, "Benefit Sanctions Cost More Than They Save,

aren't at heart exercises in fiscal conservativism or austerity. There is a definite gleefulness in the minutiae of demands they make and the suffering they impose. This is fully ripe neoliberalism—as a consumer, the individual is sovereign and their every desire (provided they have the necessary disposable income) fawned over. But, as a worker, or potential worker, they must submit to a punitive, disciplinary regime. The dark side of the subordination to wage labour is just as important as the shimmering promise of freedom. The recalcitrant must be forced to be free.

## The Insight of the Outsider

Milgram's agentic state is, in my opinion, one of the most illuminating discoveries of social science in the last 40 years. There is something inherently subversive about simply asking why people are obedient to authority. Indeed, Peter Kropotkin had cited the lack of "obedience to any authority" as one of the essential qualities of anarchism in his famous *Encyclopedia Britannica* definition. Yet Milgram was not a noted political radical. He was (in modern American terminology) a liberal—he opposed the Vietnam War and was in favour of nuclear disarmament but the conclusions he

National Audit Office Finds," *Huffington Post UK*, 30 November 2016; Oliver Wright, "DWP fit-to-work assessments cost more than they save, report reveals," *Independent*, 8 January 2016. The only satisfactory conclusion is that, to the instigators of these "reforms," the psychological effect, or perhaps the outcome of forcing poor and sick people into the unknown of the precarious labour market, is worth the extra cost.

drew from his experiment were, as we shall see, depressingly conservative. Neither was he a philosopher, a political scientist or an economist. Had he been any of those, it is difficult to imagine that he would have stumbled across the insights that he did. He needed a sideways perspective—in his case gleaned from social psychology—to examine with fresh eyes a process which happens millions of times a day in the modern world—the merging of unique personalities into institutional grooves that are accepted as legitimate because they are "part of the world." According to his biographer, Milgram shone a light on "the unexpected power of certain *invisible* features of situations" and the "unverbalized social rules and norms operating within them."[49] Milgram himself characterised his approach as honing in on "the person influenced by social forces while often believing in his or her independence of them."[50]

By contrast, neoliberalism and its academic twin, neo-classical economics, focus unerringly on the surface, idealised features of situations. Because direct coercion is not present at the moment the labour contract is agreed, wage labour, in the neoliberal worldview, becomes the epitome of a voluntary, consensual transaction. After it is signed, employers don't exercise command over workers—they jointly "determine the course of events." According to a major plank of neo-classical economics—the theory of marginal productivity—the wage workers receive is mathematically equal to their

---

49  Thomas Blass, *The Man Who Shocked the World: The Life and Legacy of Stanley Milgram* (Basic Books, 2004), xxiii.

50  Ibid., 290.

contribution. In a free market economy, wages (and rent) are precisely (and conveniently) what they should be—workers get their just deserts and have no cause to feel exploited. In other words, what workers receive in actuality—the surface outcome—exactly corresponds to their underlying input into the production process, which is invisible to the naked eye.[51]

However, to get to the reality of any situation, you have to distrust surface appearances. Karl Marx rooted his entire analysis of the capitalist system on a "social process that goes on behind the backs of the producers." The price of products is different from their real value, but this value, dependent on the quantity of labour, raw materials and machinery in production, cannot be calculated in advance. The rate of profit has a tendency to fall over time but this is an entirely unconscious process—because businesses, in a market system, are in a life or death competitive struggle with each other, they are compelled to steadily replace workers with machinery. As labour is the ultimate source of value or profit, this inexorable process leads to economic crisis. And most famously, Marx asserted that the ostensibly equal exchange of working for a wage hides the extraction of "surplus value," since the capitalist always pays less than the full value of

---

51 Naturally, this is a bogus claim. It is, for example, impossible to justify the average £5.3 million annual salaries of FTSE 100 corporate chief executives in the UK on the basis of their putative contribution to productivity, which cannot be worked out. It is equally impossible to isolate the contribution of other workers. See Chapter 11 of Moshe Adler's *Economics for the Rest of Us* (The New Press, 2010), 143-150.

what the worker produces. The success or failure of social transformation seemed to hinge on the majority of people becoming conscious of these clandestine operations.

Adam Smith, who preceded Marx, and is considered to be the father of market economics, believed the value of wages to be the result of a perpetual struggle between "masters" and "workmen," though one which takes place in half light. Though actions by workers to "combine" occur in the full glare of publicity and usually lead to the "ruin of the ringleaders," Smith observed, collusion by employers to keep down wages, though much more common, is concealed. "Masters are always and everywhere in a sort of tacit, but constant and uniform combination, not to raise the wages of labour above their actual rate ... we seldom, indeed, hear of this combination because it is the usual, and one may say, natural state of things, which nobody ever hears of," he wrote.[52]

Milgram, too, eviscerated the idealised story of his field—the narrative of unbroken human volition and altruism. He disputed the practically universal but "seriously distorted view of the determinants of human action." Almost everyone expected the subjects of Milgram's experiment to refuse to obey and almost everyone, as it turned out, was wrong. Many appeared almost programmed to act as agents for the wishes of authority despite recoiling from what they were being asked to do. But Milgram's explanation for why so many found the agentic state impossible to resist was superficial and conservative. He blamed the presence of obedience on "a fatal flaw nature has designed into us." A person's

---

52  Adam Smith, *The Wealth of Nations* (Penguin, 1999), 169-170.

conscience, which inhibits aggressive impulses, is diminished upon entering a "hierarchical structure," he claimed. But humans, not being solitary animals, inevitably function within such hierarchical structures—to Milgram they are synonymous with organisation and coordination in social life. There is a clear "evolutionary bias" to this analysis—evolution has preordained that people willingly accept the strictures of authority, that they readily enter the "agentic state" for the greater good. "Behaviour, like any other of man's characteristics," said Milgram "has through successive generations been shaped by the requirements of survival." In this, humans are not vastly different from animals, though in human societies, authority is "mediated by symbols rather than direct contests of physical strength." In fact, Milgram takes the human/animal analogy a good deal further:

> When a wolf pack brings down its prey, for example, the dominant wolf enjoys first privileges, followed by the next dominant one, and so on down the line. Each member's acknowledgement of its place in the hierarchy stabilises the pack. The same is true of human groups: internal harmony is ensured when all members accept the status assigned to them.[53]

Whatever Milgram's deep misgivings about the effects of obedience to authority, he regarded it as an unavoidable evolutionary adaptation. This is a fundamentally conservative standpoint. While neoliberals celebrate obedience as a mark of freedom, provided it has been elicited by contract and

---

53  Milgram, *Obedience to Authority*, 126.

not coercion, Milgram saw it as a dangerous but inescapable companion of human life. Social stability, in fact, requires that people "accept the status assigned to them." It is critical, as few evidently are, to be aware of the subterranean power of obedience, but you cannot hope to eradicate it and should not try. Thus, to Milgram, the only safeguard against the deformity of obedience is an attitude of unceasing scepticism towards power.[54]

54  Ibid., 188-189.

# Chapter Two

# Is Obedience Natural?

## Social Ecology and the Evolutionary Mystification of Obedience

Stanley Milgram thus was resigned to obedience. In the same way as we have evolved to walk on two legs and see only a limited spectrum of light, we too have evolved to disregard our conscience when authority demands that we obey. A potential for obedience, he contended, is the prerequisite for social organisation and because organisation is essential for survival "such a capacity was bred into the organism through the extended operation of evolutionary processes."[1]

---

1    Milgram, *Obedience to Authority*, 26.

Such a view has an impressive pedigree. Obedience was one of the qualities that Charles Darwin believed gave particular human tribes in primordial times an "immense advantage" over other tribes. It was part of a collection of moral attributes (including patriotism, courage and the willingness of individual members to sacrifice themselves for the common good) that facilitated their "success" over less cohesive rival groups and generated an increase in the "standard of morality" everywhere. Such a process, he asserted, was natural selection in action.[2]

But an alternative explanation is possible—that the equation of command and obedience is not written in our genes, but rather has been instilled over centuries of rule, by humans over other humans. The form has altered— obedience has been embodied in priestly control, monarchies, aristocracies, lord/serf, master/slave and capitalist/worker antinomies and totalitarian autocracies. But the essence of the superordinate/subordinate division is constant.

For virtually all of civilised history, the vast majority of human beings have existed in a state of profound unfreedom. The chains may have taken the form of outright slavery, debt bondage to a landlord, feudalism (under which the serf had to perform unpaid labour for their lord or give up a proportion of their produce), indentured servitude, or more recently, inescapable wage labour. However, all rest on a relationship of command and obedience and, moreover, the legitimacy and inevitability of such a psychological

---

2   Charles Darwin, *The Descent of Man* (Shrine Classics, 1871), 66.

arrangement. It is therefore not surprising that in Milgram's obedience experiments many subjects, heirs to this vast historical legacy, could not resist slipping into a state where they become a mere agent for the wishes of an authority figure, overriding their often deep aversion for the content of the acts themselves.

However, history, no matter how deeply ingrained can, unlike biological traits, be transcended. According to the social ecologist Murray Bookchin, we cannot hope to free ourselves unless we become aware of our own history. "To a large extent," he said, "the history of a phenomenon is the phenomenon. We are, in a real sense, everything that existed before us and, in turn, we can eventually become vastly more than we are." And human history, or rather what is condescendingly referred to as "prehistory," does not support the contention that obedience is a natural state of affairs for human beings. Bookchin examined the outlook of what he termed "organic society"—hunter-gatherer or scavenging bands that existed for the thousands of years before agriculture took hold—and found no glimmer of the reflexes of command and obedience that stain later civilised cultures. By contrast, Bookchin observed, organic societies practiced complete parity and equality between individuals, age groups and sexes. They were founded on the principle of the "irreducible minimum"—the "inalienable right" of everyone in the community to food, shelter and clothing, "irrespective of the amount of work contributed by the individual to the acquisition of the means of life."[3] These tribal societies also eschewed any notion of ownership, preferring the practice of "usufruct," whereby the resources of the community belonged to the person using them for as long as s/he required them. Anyone was entitled to use land, orchards, tools or weapons if they were lying idle. "Things were available to individuals and families of a community because they were needed," writes Bookchin, "not because they were owned or created by the labour of a possessor."[4] Moreover, these preliterate societies consciously compensated for the difficulties faced by older members or those suffering from ill health. "Often," writes Bookchin "special 'privileges' were allowed to individuals who were burdened by infirmities to equalize their situations with respect to more endowed members of the community." The societies were governed by an outlook of mutual respect that did not cast people into superordinate and subordinate roles. Such "an ethics of complementarity" did not just apply to other people, but eschewed any thought of dominating the natural world as well.

Organic society was much more than an evanescent spark in human development. Human "behavioural modernity"-symbolic communication, planning, art and music, clothing, bodily decoration, the construction of complex shelters and the cultivation of technology (bows and arrows for example)—

---

3   Murray Bookchin, *The Ecology of Freedom: The Emergence and Dissolution of Hierarchy* (AK Press, 2005), 123. The source is the 20th century American anthropologist Paul Radin.

4   Murray Bookchin, *Remaking Society* (Black Rose Books, 1989), 50.

begins to appear around 45,000 years ago, although, in genetic and anatomical terms, Homo Sapiens are much older, dating back maybe 200,000 years. This explosion in creativity and inventiveness—known as the "Human Revolution"—even extended to mass producing tools using rudimentary "assembly line" techniques—the kind of process thought to be unique to the Industrial Revolution of the 18th and 19th centuries. Hunter-gatherers were thus fully human, not some unfinished prototype of modern humanity. Whatever the unquestioned tyrannies of ancient empires and modern civilisations, they do not tell the whole human story. Far from it, for approximately 9/10ths of their existence, modern humans have inhabited egalitarian, non-hierarchical, non-obedient societies.

## The Unresolved Paradox of Early Humanity

But perhaps things are not so neat. Bookchin, in common with other radical anthropologists, has been accused of romanticising early human societies, downplaying their violence—internally and towards other tribes—and basing sweeping assertions of egalitarianism on scant evidence. Recent archaeological research has unearthed evidence suggesting that Upper Paleolithic hunter-gatherer societies were far more stratified than first thought. Grand burials—for example the 25,000-year-old grave of a middle-aged man adorned with ivory bracelets and beads found near present-day Moscow—have fuelled suspicions that inherited wealth and power stretch right back to human beginnings. While monumental constructions—witness the 15,000-year-old "mammoth houses" comprising hides covering a frame of tusks found from Poland to Ukraine—imply large-scale recruitment and mobilisation of labour. Bookchin himself has been arraigned for leaning too heavily on 20th century ethnographic studies of tribal peoples, such as the Native American Hopi and Wintu and the Ihalmiut Eskimos of modern Canada, who have survived into the present. This does seem to be an inescapable limitation of "ethnographic analogy"—the practice of reading back into the distant past from observation of the behaviour of still existing traditional, tribal societies. As has been well attested (for example by Claude Lévi-Strauss), it is hazardous to try and reconstruct the archaeological past from observation of contemporary hunter-gatherers. They invariably live in proximity to modern industrialised societies and may supplement their "hunter-gatherer" lifestyle by farming. In short, the hunter-gatherers of 40,000 years ago may have been very different to their modern cousins.

However, it should be stressed that Bookchin never succumbed to the temptation to eulogise primordial society—to pluck it from the perilous material conditions in which it was engulfed, or, as was the case with primitivists in the 1990s, the wish to mimic "Paleolithic consciousness." He freely acknowledged (again largely based on 20th century ethnography) that hunter-gatherer tribes curtailed personal freedom when necessary, beat or murdered threatening individuals, hunted some species to extinction and could be senselessly cruel to animals they captured. Bookchin was not trying to revive the Noble Savage as a counterpoint to modern decay. He flatly denied that the hunter-gatherer epoch constituted any kind of golden age for humanity. While paying due respect to the cooperative spirit of our Paleolithic forebears, he regarded subsequent developments such as the idea of a universal *humanitas*, writing (which when prised from the control of society's rulers is a force for democratisation), urban living and science unequivocal advances over the parochialism and "innocence" of the tribe. His aim was, rather, to "pick out" the "experiences and experiments" of organic society that were "particularly relevant for our times."[5]

Whether or not humanity ever existed in a state of primal unity—whether the virtues of Bookchin's organic society were universal or sporadic—will probably never been known for certain. However, Bookchin's conclusions about early humans were not merely unverifiable speculations. In addition to utilising ethnographic studies, he made highly plausible inferences from accepted facts and realities which would, in all likelihood, have predisposed early human societies towards mutual aid and egalitarianism, and away from hierarchy, certainly away from individualism. These include the prolonged dependence (much longer than with non-human animals) of human infants, the collective nature of child-care involving siblings, kin groups and the wider community, the sharing of food and responsibility towards the infirm and the unarguable need for survival in an unforgiving environment. As he concludes:

---

5    Bookchin, *Ecology of Freedom*, 56, 78.

early human association must have fostered a strong predisposition for *interdependence* among members of a group—not the "rugged individualism" we associate with independence ... The idea that people are dependent upon each other for the good life, indeed, for survival, followed from the prolonged dependence of the young upon adults. Independence, not to mention competition, would have seemed utterly alien, if not bizarre, to a creature reared over many years in a largely dependent condition. Care for others would have been seen as the perfectly natural outcome of a highly acculturated being that was, in turn, clearly in need of extended care. Our modern version of individualism, more precisely, of egotism, would have cut across the grain of early solidarity and mutual aid—traits, I may add, without which such a physically fragile animal like a human being could hardly have survived as an adult, much less as a child.[6]

---

6   Bookchin. *Remaking Society*, 28. These insights utterly contradict the contention of classical liberals like Von Mises and Hayek that primitive man always had the latent urge to exchange goods and buy and sell services, but needed modern capitalism to give vent to such desires. In *The Great Transformation* (1944), Karl Polanyi pointed out that Adam Smith's famous assertion of the innate human desire to "barter, truck and exchange" was "almost entirely apocryphal." Rather until the demise of European feudalism, food or goods were either given up for communal consumption (as in tribal societies), stored and distributed (as in ancient kingdoms and empires) or formed part of a reciprocal gift economy (as in many contemporary indigenous societies). But in the "short run"

In fact, recent attempts have been made to combine the insights of anthropology with those of archaeology and thus enable more informed judgements about the political and economic configurations of prehistoric humanity to be made. David Wengrow, Professor of Comparative Archaeology at University College London has collaborated with the aforementioned David Graeber, Professor of Comparative Anthropology at the London School of Economics, to examine the "origins of inequality."[7] Their conclusions are interesting. Rather than being inherently egalitarian or hierarchical, they assert that Upper Paleolithic hunter-gatherers (i.e. from 40,000 years BP) consciously alternated between political forms, and did so according to the seasons—and in the Ice Age conditions of the time, the environment was highly seasonal. The "same population," they say "might experience entirely different systems of economic relations,

---

worldview of economists and historians everything in the past was assumed to be paving the way for the system that was to reign supreme from the19th century onwards, the market economy, "irrespective of other tendencies which were temporarily submerged." Even though the idea of a marketing psychology as a timeless and universal attribute of human nature has been exposed as a myth, it still exhibits a tenacious hold on both public and academic consciousness.

7    David Wengrow and David Graeber, "Farewell to the 'childhood of man': Ritual, seasonality and the origins of inequality," *Journal of the Royal Anthropological Institute*, 21:3 (2015), 597-619. In 2018, they released another collaborative article: "How to change the course of human history," Eurozine, 2 March 2018.

family structure and political life at different times of year."[8] A coercive authority might reign in winter, only to be dissolved in summer when the tribe dispersed into smaller groups. But, significantly, at no time was rule entrenched—a person who wielded power for a period would be subject to it at a later stage. This led to the awareness that "*no* social order was immutable: that everything was at least potentially open to negotiation, subversion and change."[9]

Certainly, the accumulating evidence indicates that, as humanity made the fateful step from a nomadic to a sedentary, initially horticultural, existence—a process that took thousands of years and even today has not been fully accomplished—hierarchy did not simply overpower egalitarianism. Quite the contrary, in moving from a dependence on "man the hunter," egalitarianism was likely strengthened. The building sites and graves of late Stone Age villages give no indication of social inequality. In Europe, Neolithic villages consisted of two or three dozen 30-40 metre long timber longhouses that housed extended family groups; a communal arrangement that seems to rule out the possibility that a nascent élite appropriated the fruits of the community's labour. According to Bookchin, the surpluses that began to be generated by food production would have been distributed "without transgressing the community's norms of usufruct, complementarity and the irreducible minimum."[10] Neolithic fixed soil communities were most likely "matricentric"— horticulture or gardening was probably developed by women

---


8   Graeber and Wengrow, "Farewell," 613.

9   Ibid.

10  Bookchin, *Ecology of Freedom*, 142.

who also were responsible for cross-fertilizing wild species into domestic crops, such as wheat or barley. Their descent was also matrilineal. Patriarchy—the domination of men over women—so marked in the warrior-led societies of the Bronze Age and the civilisations of classical antiquity had yet to take root.

However, it is important to be aware that reality was far looser and more complicated than the stages that history has subsequent imposed on early human development. These stages presuppose an agricultural revolution that generated sufficient material surpluses to enable an urban revolution to take place. The first cities could support a non-productive élite of priests, administrators and soldiers who formed the backbone of the despotic empires of antiquity. In truth, the first known city in history—the 9,000-year-old Çatal Hüyük in modern-day Turkey—was populated by late Paleolithic hunter-gatherers and not food cultivators—who nourished themselves largely through the hunting of game and the harvesting of undomesticated plants. A vast city by ancient standards, sustaining a population of 7,000 over several centuries, Çatal Hüyük was strikingly egalitarian. It had no discernible social classes, royalty or religious hierarchies as well as giving equal social status to men and women. Çatal Hüyük was also not the precursor to greater urbanisation—it was simply deserted by its inhabitants after hundreds of years of occupancy.

Similarly, horticulture or farming was assumed to be indelibly associated with Neolithic village life. However, as is becoming increasingly evident to archaeologists, nomadic Paleolithic hunter-gatherers frequently practiced farming but merely as one part of a hunting, fishing and food gathering "economy." Food cultivation was taking place at least 18,000 years ago (in Egypt next to the Nile), at the same time as the Magdalenian peoples in Western Europe were hunting bison and painting in caves. All this indicates that the reasons behind the emergence of civilisation are much more complicated than first thought.

But emerge it did, in all corners of the world—China, South Asia, the Americas, the Near East and Africa. Sumer, in modern-day southern Iraq, is considered to be the earliest civilisation and is the place where writing began. Beginning around 5,000 BC and lasting over three millennia, Sumer at its height consisted of 27 city-states clustered around the Tigris-Euphrates delta. War-like, ruled by kings and presided over by priests and officials, Sumerian cities exhibited all the hierarchical blights that have come to be associated with civilisation—they had slaves and workers, sexual and economic inequality and even colonies. But, fascinatingly, Sumer did not begin that way. According to archaeologist Henri Frankfort, originally and for many generations, Sumerian cities were governed by "equalitarian" assemblies.[11] These assemblies possessed "freedom to an uncommon degree" and were so

---

11  Henri Frankfort, *The Birth of Civilization in the Near East* (Doubleday Anchor Books, 1956), 78. He says of the Sumerian assembly, "It is as well to recognise the extraordinary character of this urban form of political organization," and compares its assertion of the sovereignty of the citizenry with political expressions that developed many thousands of years later, such as those of Ancient Athens, Renaissance Italy and the Hanseatic League.

apprehensive about infringing ancient tribal unity they did not impose the will of the majority on the minority, preferring to deliberate until unanimity was reached. As the cities expanded and disputes over land and water rights escalated, hierarchy started to vie with egalitarianism. "Lugal," or "great men," were granted emergency powers to wage war against neighbouring cities but their tenure was limited. When the emergency subsided, power would revert to the assembly once again. However, as destructive and futile wars became incessant, the great man system solidified into a permanent and new social form—kingship.[12]

## Humanity's Two Natures

Hierarchy was thus not "bred into the organism." For most of human existence hierarchy has been a partial and transitory, rather than universal, feature of life. Indeed, it's been rejected for millennia at a time or been forced to wrestle with egalitarianism for supremacy for long periods. Its erratic presence is a sign that it is not an evolutionary adaptation but belongs to a qualitatively different realm; that of human social history. Incontestably, hierarchy is now virtually universal and has been for thousands of years, though its forms have waxed and waned. But this very ubiquity deceptively marks it as an indelible aspect of human nature.

---

12  In the *Epic of Gilgamesh*, the story of the eponymous Sumerian King of Uruk who ruled around 2700 BC, Gilgamesh still had consult to an assembly of the people and the elders before he embarked on a course of action that might lead to war.

These inequalities and oppressions might appear to be the malign offspring of humanity's animal evolution—and thus eternally fixed in the same way that a lion's compulsion to hunt antelopes is simply a part of its being—but they are, in reality, cultural developments. These unfolding ways of living can be denoted "cultural evolution" but they have followed qualitatively different—and much more rapid—pathways than humanity's genetic evolution. Thus, there is a point at which natural evolution ends and conscious, uniquely human, experimentation with social forms begins, or to be more accurate, the latter branches off from the former. Muddying the waters between the two can, and frequently does, lead to the misguided conclusion that established patterns of human interaction are immutably preordained by "nature." In grasping for an explanation for obedience, this is precisely how Milgram cornered himself.

Making this distinction does not require discounting the significance of humanity's genetic evolution, but merely asserts that it is woefully ill equipped to explain the meandering course of human history and the diversity of social forms and cultures that people have created. Bookchin—in common with another noted non-Marxist Left thinker, Noam Chomsky—did not subscribe to the notion that human nature is a *tabula rasa* on which is inscribed whatever historically determined social relations exist at any given time. In contrast, he paid due respect to what he termed humanity's "first nature." First nature is a strictly biological realm. Human beings are clearly part of first nature—they are mammals and primates and have "primal natural urges."[13] However, as a consequence of *natural evolution itself*, humans are also driven to intervene in the natural world to secure the means of life. It is part of their "animality" to alter the world around them. "People change first nature by virtue of their *naturally* endowed capacities to think conceptually, to create extra-biological tools and machines," said Bookchin, "and to do this with a high degree of collective organization and intentionality that is profoundly different from the behaviour and abilities of nonhuman beings."[14]

But the character of this "collective organization" is not specified by first nature. While animals—when they are social—form largely fixed, genetically programmed communities or herds, humans live in societies. Societies are part of *second nature*, the arena of conscious, uniquely human, open-ended experimentation, and are not governed by the blind imperatives of natural selection. Societies are deliberately designed and thus constructed around highly mutable institutions. A cursory glance at history shows the sheer variety of societies that humans have fashioned, encompassing tribal associations, slave states, feudal arrangements, empires, capitalist formations, mixed economies, authoritarian and totalitarian regimes, absolute monarchies, theocracies, republics, representative democracies, direct democracies, and communist systems. If "being determines consciousness," as Marxian theory would have it, this is so for animals but not necessarily for humans who possess the freedom to experiment.

---

13   Bookchin, *Remaking Society*, 30.

14   Bookchin, *Ecology of Freedom*, 32.

Such experimentation is the exclusive province of second nature. Second nature embodies cultural traditions and innovation, a complex language, conceptual powers and the capacity to purposefully and dramatically reshape the surrounding environment. It is both a product of first nature—the human mind's ability to think conceptually can be traced back through millions of years of genetic evolution—and has immense ramifications quite apart from it. This division has great affinities with Chomsky's delineation of human nature. Chomsky, whose concept of Universal Grammar presupposes an innate capacity to learn a language, disputes that humans are merely "empty organisms." "We may think of human nature," he asserts, as a "system of 'mental organs' … that provides for a unique form of intelligence that manifests itself in human language; in our unique capacity to develop a concept of number and abstract space; to construct scientific theories in certain domains; to create systems of art, myth and ritual, to interpret human actions [and] to develop and comprehend certain systems of social institutions." These innate abilities, he says, have allowed the human species to "create the conditions under which it will live to an extent without significant analogue in the natural world." Human nature is thus both bounded and, within those bounds, open to immense variation and experimentation. Or, as Chomsky puts it, "humans are unique in the natural world in that they have history, cultural diversity and cultural evolution."[15]

15  Quotes are from the 1976 essay, "Equality," published in Noam Chomsky, *The Chomsky Reader* (Pantheon, 1987), 194-198. "A human nature does exist," said Bookchin, "but it seems to consist

## Hierarchy is Social

To Bookchin, therefore, hierarchy is a "strictly social term, exclusively characteristic of second nature."[16] Etymologically, hierarchy derives from an ancient Greek word meaning "rule of the high priest" (or priestess). Hierarchy embodies both the power to command and the duty to obey and can be observed at work in its original backdrop of organised religion (which goes much, much further back than Christianity, Islam or Buddhism) or, to give a few obvious examples, in corporations, government bureaucracies and the military. But precisely because of its uniquely human—and therefore contingent origins—hierarchy is prone to zoological mystification. Spurious analogies are drawn between human social arrangements and genetically imprinted dominance and submission behaviour in the animal world.[17] The existence of alpha and beta male gorillas, queen bees and worker drones, feeding prerogatives in hyena packs or a pecking order among chickens is used to justify why some people own society while others are owned by it. "What we normally call domination in nature," says Bookchin "is a *human projection* of highly organized systems

of proclivities and potentialities that become increasingly defined by the instillation of social needs." See Bookchin, *Ecology of Freedom*, 186.

16  Bookchin, *Ecology of Freedom*, 24-25.

17  The technical term for this is theriomorphism—the ascription of animal characteristics to humans. Its opposite is anthropomorphism, the much more commonly noted attribution of human characteristics to animals. Both are misguided.

of *social* command and obedience onto highly idiosyncratic, individual, and asymmetrical forms of often mildly coercive behaviour in animal communities."[18]

The latest personification of this erstwhile and seemingly irresistible tendency is Canadian psychologist and "classical liberal" Jordan Peterson. He claims that lobsters and human beings, despite diverging in evolutionary terms at least 350 million years ago, both exist in hierarchies of authority, which are, in fact, "older than trees."[19] Extreme economic inequality among humans has the same ultimate cause as the certainty that lobsters will fight over who has access to the best hiding places—a perpetual striving for dominance and survival that only a small minority can win. "It's winner-take-all in the lobster world, just as it is in human societies," writes Peterson, "where the top 1 percent have as much loot as the bottom 50 percent—and where the richest eighty-five people have as much as the bottom three and a half billion."[20] Hierarchies—or what Peterson dubs the "brutal principle of unequal distribution"—are thus imbued with a biological imprimatur; "it's inevitable," he insists, "that there will be continuity in the way that animals and human beings organise their structures."[21] The dominance hierarchy

---

18   Bookchin, Remaking Society, 33.

19   See Jordan Peterson, "God and Hierarchies of Authority," Lecture, 30 May 2017 (the segment on Darwin and lobsters is available at youtube.com/watch?v=xw1m87XsMgI&t=187s).

20   Jordan Peterson, *12 Rules for Life: An Antidote for Chaos* (Allen Lane, 2018), 8.

21   See interview with Cathy Newman on *Channel 4 News*

is a "near eternal aspect of the environment," he claims, and social and economic systems such as capitalism are merely "a consequence of its unchanging existence."[22] The implication of all such claims is that it is not only futile to try and dismantle naturally ordained hierarchies but actively dangerous since it involves trying to suppress the eternal verities of human nature. Only tyranny will result.

Humans are, in fact, the only animals that exercise choice and diversity in how they "organise their structures" (in contrast, for example, to lobsters which have replicated the same structure for hundreds of millions of years). Human social structures and hierarchies have a life of their own quite apart from the personalities of the individuals who inhabit them. They are *institutionalised*—founded on legal codes, bureaucracies and corporate hierarchies—not the outcome of the way individuals interact with each other. Humans can be dominant, confident, aggressive, inhibited, submissive, gregarious or aloof—and all stations in-between. Although these behaviours can reflect the balance of power and wealth between élite and subordinate groups they do not determine the nature of social structures. As has been amply demonstrated, low status groups are more prone to depression—and physical ill health—than those higher up the social hierarchy.[23] But changing those symptoms and

---

in the UK, 16 January 2018 (available at youtube.com/ watch?v=aMcjxSThD54&t=870s).

22  Peterson, *12 Rules*, 14.

23  "Pressure and stress affects people more at the bottom than the top. This is because their lives are more subject to uncertainty

endeavouring to alter individual behaviour will not influence the existence or character of the hierarchies within which people lead their lives.

This crucial difference between human and animal structures can be seen through the behaviour of Peterson's favourite crustacean. He is quite enamoured of the revelation that anti-depressants can be successfully administered to lobsters—a defeated, hunched lobster, low in serotonin, can be perked up and readied for battle again by giving it Prozac. It will "advance on former victors and fight longer and harder." Despite the evolutionary gulf that separates them, humans and lobsters share basic neuro-chemistry says Peterson: "The drugs prescribed to depressed human beings, which are selective serotonin reuptake inhibitors, have much the same chemical and behavioural effect."[24] However, in contrast to the revived lobster, the mass prescribing of anti-depressants that has taken place in the developed world since they were first introduced in the late 1980s—by 2004 Prozac had been prescribed to 50 million people—has not made the slightest impact on social structures or made those structures more permeable to people of low social rank. The same period that has seen the wholesale dispensing of anti-depressants, undoubtedly one of great business success stories of the

---

(e.g. threats of unemployment and related poverty); because they have fewer resources to fall back on (e.g. savings) and because they lack the power to make themselves heard." Michael Haynes and Rumy Husan, *A Century of State Murder? Death and Policy in Twentieth-Century Russia* (Pluto Press, 2001), 22.

24 Ibid., 7.

last thirty years, has also witnessed sharp declines in social mobility in the US and UK.[25] Rather than opening up careers and better incomes to people previously shut out from them, they have instead simply relieved the pain induced by increasingly segregated and mapped out lives.

Social classes and social strata are, in Bookchin's description, "made of sterner stuff" than individual behavioural traits. But that does not mean they are impervious to change. As history shows, society can be radically altered by popular revolution, wars or incremental developments such as progressive taxation and social security. The ruling classes of ancient empires, like the Egyptian, lived in mortal fear of the "black redistribution" by an enraged peasantry, the desecration of hierarchical order and the descent into chaos. Modern civilisations have been haunted by a quite rational fear of revolution—an unease that has not abated in contemporary times. Precisely because hierarchy is social and thus susceptible to change, it has to be actively defended—mentally as well as physically. Human societies, said Bookchin, are always "clothed in ideologies." An awareness, however dim, of the possibility of the world turning upside

-----

25  See for example, Jonathan Davis and Bhaskar Mazumder, *The Decline in Intergenerational Mobility after 1980*, working paper, Federal Reserve Bank of Minneapolis, March 2017. Or the UK's Social Mobility Commission which reported in April 2019 that "social mobility has stagnated over the last four years at virtually all life stages," with entry into professional occupations largely dependent on parents' careers. (See: https://www.theguardian.com/society/2019/apr/30/social-mobility-in-uk-virtually-stagnant-since-2014).

down, leads to an urge to protect the social order against the "smoldering potentiality for revolt" from below.[26]

## The Thread of Obedience

If hierarchy and its ideology of unthinking obedience are not rooted in biology the question arises how did they develop? Even the most egalitarian organic society, said Bookchin, is not homogenous. Everyday roles tend to be determined by sex, age and lineage. But though the sexes complement each other economically, the young and old do not. Living in fear of being killed or expelled in times of famine, elders set themselves up as indispensable repositories of wisdom and experts in the arts of hunting and food gathering; necessary roles in societies lacking a written language. Such stature can be observed in the influence of councils of elders and in the ancestor-worship common in tribal societies, and betray a state of mind in which the young habitually defer to the old. These non-institutionalised mentalities are not in themselves disruptive to early egalitarianism but social power begins to crystallise in the form of the shaman—invariably an older, usually male, member of the tribe. By interpreting the meaning of dreams, sudden storms or comets in the night sky, shamans acquire status and material privileges. They become spiritual leaders. But this kind of power is only available to the select few. It is a carefully guarded sanctum not open to most members of the community.

---

26  Quotes in this paragraph are from Bookchin, *Ecology of Freedom*, 95, 24, 195.

Shamans formed alliances with older, respected members of the tribe as a protection against popular anger when their magic did not have the desired effect. Often these allies were so-called "big men"—the most capable hunters and warriors who commanded public admiration and gave away gifts in "potlach" ceremonies. Tribal chiefs were invariably big men but as chiefs they still didn't have formal powers, merely dispensed advice. However, the chief may begin to undermine the egalitarianism of preliterate societies either by asserting the supremacy of his clan group over all others, or by adopting strangers as military companions, forming "companies" that were, in essence, incipient monarchies and aristocracies. The "big man" was an autocrat in the making.[27]

The shaman was the precursor of the high priest who dominated the first civilisations. The temples or "ziggurats" of Sumer were controlled by priests. In the three storey ziggurat, the priests lived on the second floor and administered the workforce—tool makers, weavers or stone cutters—who were housed on the bottom floor. The top floor was reserved for deities—statues of the gods were placed on this level. Only the high priest was allowed on the third tier and, according to imprisoned Kurdish leader Abdullah Öcalan, this level was kept extremely secret.

---

27  The chief may assert the supremacy of his kin group over others, thereby ascribing royal or dynastic status to an entire clan or, as with the Sumerian King Gilgamesh, adopt a stranger as his "companion." Either way the egalitarian norms of preliterate society are undermined and the roots of monarchy and aristocracy laid. See Bookchin, *Remaking Society*, 59-60.

"Society was told that it was on the third floor that the high priest continuously met and talked with the gods. Thus, anyone wanting to hear the word of god had to listen to the high priest. He was the only authorised spokesperson of God."[28] The high priests, unlike their shaman forebears, also explicitly linked the idea of God with that of sin and punishment, thus instilling the notion of obedience. The Sumerian priest is the first example of institutionalised power—the authority to command and the expectation of obedience that stem from the social role itself, rather than individual charisma, talent, personal authority or dominance. Over time in Sumerian cities, the number of priests, and priestesses, grew immensely. They became a new sacred class—"god's deputies"—forming an urban administrative élite under the leadership of the high priest.[29]

But Sumer's priesthood had a rival. Their intellectual power was confronted by the physical and military power of "great men" or lugal—the individuals chosen to wage war and who, in time, became Sumer's Kings and formed a dynasty (rule perpetuated through the succession of the son to the father's throne). These were the descendants of the tribal "big men," the belligerent warriors of early human society who were now emerging as a fully-fledged élite. Thus began the long rivalry—lasting several millennia which in many parts of the world is still not over—between

---

28  Abdullah Öcalan, *Manifesto for a Democratic Civilization, Volume 1: The Age of Masked Gods and Disguised Kings* (New Compass Press, 2015), 100. The analysis of Sumerian society is on pages 96-110.

29  Ibid., 100.

theological and secular or political power. "New gods were constructed and the priests were reduced to deputies of the political leaders," writes Öcalan. "They still played an important role, but increasingly lost their power and became mere propagandists of the system."[30] Sumer's God-Kings also originate the concept of private property and inheritance. Though the priest-run ziggurat system, in contrast to Neolithic village society, was exploitative, it was still basically a communal economy—workers were paid in roughly equal rations. With private property, huge inequality in wealth was established.

The incipient exploitation of Sumer was fully consummated in the Egyptian pharaoh states that followed—the Egyptian New Kingdom (1550 to 1070 BC) in particular was based on slavery, often swelled through prisoners captured in war, and forced labour. "In no other civilization has the unity of master and slave reached the level it had in Egypt," remarks Öcalan. The shadow of Sumer's great men can be seen in Bronze Age warrior chieftains—Homeric heroes such as Achilles, Odysseus and Agamemnon. These nobles and kings lived in fortresses. Their great wealth enabled them to build palaces, acquire arms, buy the loyalty of mercenaries and wage incessant plundering wars. They formed dynasties and exerted a patriarchal tyranny over their wives and families. Their status grew out of a seigniorial economy—the mass of people lived as serfs, undertook corvée labour for their lord and herded their "considerable flocks." At this point in history, the essential components

---

30  Ibid., 108.

of hierarchy—patriarchy, social inequality, obedience and aristocratic dynasties—were all in place.[31]

## Élite Power and Episodic Sovereignty

By this stage, the egalitarianism of tribal and Neolithic village society was a vanishing memory. Although a "shadowy Assembly of the People" still existed in Agamemnon's time, to be consulted on important occasions, it seems to have had very little power.[32] And this places in sharp relief what hierarchy actually was. Some system of authority, said Milgram, is a basic requirement of all communal living. Hunter-gatherer and Neolithic village communities were intensely communal societies—far more communal in fact than our individualist and atomised aggregations. Discipline, authority and a division of labour were not

---

31  This fact does invite the question of what came first—patriarchy
or the domination of men by other men? In fact, the two may have
grown in tandem. In the Egyptian pharaoh states, women had equal
legal rights with men and could be called up for labour service by
the state. Yet Egypt was a highly autocratic political system that
dominated both sexes in myriad ways. In Sumer, too, although men
predominated, women could become priestesses, own businesses
and pass on property. The full flowering of patriarchy came later.
In addition, modern capitalism has an internal logic of growth
and exploitation quite separate from the domination of men over
women. For a discussion of these issues, see Janet Biehl, *Rethinking
Ecofeminist Politics* (South End Press, 1991).

32  H.D.F Kitto, *The Greeks* (Penguin, 1991), 65.

foreign concepts to them—in societies that lived on the edge of survival they were essential. But, crucially, they were never entrenched as the sole prerogative of an élite. Sumer's fledgling Kings, it will be remembered, were granted dictatorial powers only for as long as the need to wage war against a rival city existed—once the emergency passed the tribal assembly was again sovereign. But over many generations their origins became forgotten and Sumerian cities became dynastic. "The closer we come to cultures organized in bands and comparatively simple tribes" writes Bookchin in *The Ecology of Freedom,* "the more 'rule' is an ad hoc, non-institutionalized system of administration." As an example he cites Native American Crow societies. They were marked by a rotation of functions and "episodic" sovereignty—control exerted for well-defined ends, such as Bison hunts. Though it clearly existed, rule never became permanent, ingrained as the abiding and acknowledged ascendancy of one stratum of society over the rest of its members. As Bookchin remarks:

What we flippantly call "leadership" in organic societies often turns out to be guidance, lacking the usual accoutrements of command. Its "power" is functional rather than political. Chiefs, where they authentically exist and are not the mere creation of the colonizer's mind, have no true authority in the coercive sense. They are advisors, teachers and consultants, esteemed for their experience and wisdom. Whatever "power" they do have is usually confined to highly delimited tasks such as the coordination of hunts and war expeditions. It ends with the tasks to be performed. Hence, it is episodic power, not institutional; periodic, not traditional—like the "dominance" traits we encounter among primates.[33]

Wengrow and Graeber, quoted above, would doubtless demur on the point that hunter-gatherer chiefs possessed no real coercive authority. They claim that coercion and "police powers" existed among hunter-gatherers, probably when different tribes gathered together at certain times of the year. However, they also point out that authority was reversible—over the course of a year "social structures … were regularly assembled and disassembled, created and destroyed."[34] Early human societies, they insist, were quite conscious of the dangers of authoritarian power and adopted strategies to make sure it did not become ensconced. They cite, for example, early 20th century anthropologist Robert Lowie, who observed that the Native American societies of the Great Plains "rotated the clan or warrior societies that held office so that anyone holding coercive powers one year would be subject to them the next" and that the power of political leaders was deliberately circumscribed so "as to exclude the emergence of permanent structures of coercion."[35]

Manifestly, in human history, permanent structures of coercion *did* emerge and authoritarian power *was* entrenched, reaching heights of cruelty and degradation. But the other form of power—where it is shared among members

---

33  Bookchin, *Ecology of Freedom*, 122.

34  Graeber and Wengrow, "Farewell," 606.

35  Ibid.

of a community, rather than being the exclusive possession of an élite, was not simply extinguished. It led an underground existence and then erupted furiously in Ancient Athens from around the 6th century BC—and quite probably in other Hellenic poleis that allied themselves with Athens.

Athenian democracy was consciously designed to thwart entrenched élite power. It emerged as a reaction to the debt slavery of much of the population and the consequent overriding power of a few rich men. People—or even their children—could be sold to appease their creditors, or be forced into exile. So under public pressure, an enlightened ruler—Solon—cancelled the debts of the poorest and created institutions to fortify the power of the demos. A popular assembly, known as the ecclesia, which dated back to tribal times, was revived. Open to all adult male citizens, at the height of Athenian democracy the ecclesia met almost weekly and enacted the community's laws and elected its magistrates. The assembly's agenda was set by a kind of executive council, the boule, which held power when the ecclesia was not in session. The boule had 500 members—each of Athens' 10 "tribes" contributed 50 men who were chosen by lot and rotated every year. A court system—which tried all civil and penal cases apart from murder—involved 6,000 citizen jurors again chosen by sortition. Even posts in the Athenian army and navy were rotated—a person could be a general one year and a private solider the next.[36] To guard against power degenerating once again into the permanent possession of a privileged class, there was a rule that no public office could be

---

36  Kitto, *The Greeks*, 127.

held for more than one year. In addition, most public offices couldn't be held more than twice in a lifetime. Participation was encouraged through financial compensation.

Clearly Athenian democracy was exclusionary—it was closed to women, slaves and resident foreigners, who together greatly outnumbered the maybe 40,000 Athenian male citizens who could participate.[37] Nevertheless, it explicitly drew on ancestral tribal practice in its attempts, manifested in strategies like rotation and limited tenure in office, to prevent entrenched élite power developing. Often this was quite deliberate—the ecclesia was a revived tribal institution and under one of the architects of democracy, Cleisthenes, Athens and its environs were divided into ten territorially-based tribes, each with its own popular assembly. At the same time, the fact that the tribes were organised geographically, as opposed to according to family

---

37 These egregious flaws pertained to the Athenian society of the
   time, not the democratic ideas Athens pioneered. In the same
   way, the contemporary reverence for representative government,
   based on a universal franchise, is not invalidated by the fact
   that many, if not all, of the elected representative institutions
   revered today – such as the British House of Commons or
   the US Congress—were originally designed to represent a
   tiny property-owning elite and deliberately excluded the vast
   majority of society. Even—in the American case—consecrating
   chattel slavery by calculating representation in part based on the
   number of slaves.

ties, was a conscious attempt to supplant the clan-based limitations of tribal history.[38]

In other words, while it is possible to track the emergence of hierarchy, from its origins in hunter-gatherer societies to its ripening in ancient empires and beyond, it is also possible to do the opposite—to see how resistance to authoritarian power was also always consciously present in preliterate times, and despite being repressed in subsequent civilisations, was never far below the surface. In the right circumstances—despite a distance of thousands of years—it could re-emerge into the light again.

More than this, such an approach casts light on what Milgram's obedience actually is. The basic principle of Athenian democracy—"to rule and be ruled in turn"—like the episodic sovereignty of organic society, does not imply a repudiation of discipline, organisation, coordination or functional authority.[39] Rather this is a knowing condition—undertaken with explicit awareness of the intention at hand and that roles will be reversed in time. Milgram's obedience and the agentic state—where a person willingly turns him or herself into a mere instrument for carrying out the wishes of a person of higher status—is, by contrast, automatic and not reflective and so strong many find it impossible to disobey even when they are repulsed by what they are commanded to do. It is unreasoned. Rather than a timeless

---

38  See Murray Bookchin, *From Urbanization to Cities: Toward a New Politics of Citizenship* (Cassell, 1995), 70-76; and Biehl, *Rethinking Ecofeminist Politics*, 147.

39  The term "to rule and be ruled in turn" is from Kitto, *The Greeks*, 127.

flaw in human nature brought to light in a New England university campus in 1961, it is the fateful psychological consequence of institutionalising hierarchical structures as permanent and intractable.[40]

Was this dark course inevitable? A counterfactual history, says Bookchin, is conceivable. The values of the Neolithic village—care for others, usufruct and the irreducible minimum—might have carved out a different future for humanity than the one that occurred. Öcalan regards the solidarity, fraternity, maternal laws and desire for equality of Neolithic culture as reasons for its endurance over thousands of years. Moreover, the civilisations that replaced it have never been able to completely expunge its principles as these are essential for social life as such. However, the disintegration of Neolithic society and the rise of urbanised living were common to virtually all parts of the world—China, Africa, Europe, the Americas—regions that had no contact with each other. This suggests there was something inexorable about the development. And, Neolithic society, in addition to its virtues, contained disturbing elements, such as child sacrifice, which needed to be expunged. In any case, "warrior values of combat, class domination and state rule," in Bookchin's words, "were to form the basic

---

40 "I believe," wrote Milgram's biographer Thomas Blass in 2011, "that one of the most important aspects of Milgram's legacy is that, in demonstrating our extreme readiness to obey authorities, he has identified one of the universals, or constants, of human behavior, straddling time and place." Blass, "Obedience Experiments at 50."

infrastructure of all 'civilised' development."[41] This had momentous consequences for both inner and outer life.

## Hierarchy's Penetration of the Psyche

Obedience is not merely about compliance with the demands of power. As Milgram clarified, obedience and coercion are not two sides of the same coin; they are quite different things. Obedience is not engendered by pointing a gun—it is dependent on a degree of collusion with the stance of the order-giver. That is to say, the obedient subject does not have to agree with the actions they are asked to perform, but they have to agree that they ought to obey.

Thus the mental ramifications of rule are just as significant as its physical aspects. According to Bookchin, the triumph of hierarchy was never just about the imposition of material structures of oppression. The long journey from egalitarianism to hierarchy and class-based society was as much about subjective shifts, internalising command and obedience in the minds of the ruled, as it was about outward compulsion:

> The subjective shifts found expression in the emergence of a repressive sensibility and body of values—in various ways of mentalizing the entire realm of experience along lines of command and obedience. Such mentalities could very well be called *epistemologies of rule*, to use a broad philosophical term. As much as any material development, these epistemologies

---

41  Bookchin, *Remaking Society*, 77.

of rule fostered the development of patriarchy and an egoistic morality in the rulers of society; in the ruled, they fostered a psychic apparatus rooted in guilt and renunciation. Just as aggression flexes our bodies for fight or flight, so class societies organize our psychic structures for command or obedience.[42]

The traditional Marxist schema of a venal élite controlling the means of production and exploiting a begrudging and rebellious servant class was only part of the story. Even the most victimised strata in class society—chattel slaves and serfs—cooperate in a mental partition. The state's capacity for brute force was always limited, said Bookchin, the idea of a purely coercive, omnipotent state a convenient fiction. Its authority would have dissipated without the collusion of the oppressed. Command was achieved as much by the "inner voice" of obedience as by the naked power of physical violence.

This might seem a chastening and debilitating realisation as it entails relinquishing the "innocent masses/evil élites" theory of history. But, in reality, it engenders hope not despair. For the coercive power of the state has now reached such a degree of perfection, that if élite dominance throughout history were founded on nothing more than superior firepower, then the future really would be, in Orwell's famous phrase, "a boot stamping on a human face forever." However, if it has also always rested on a degree, however submerged, of cooperation, then the future is not determined. Obedience tendered can be obedience withdrawn. The history of the

---

42  Bookchin, *Ecology of Freedom*, 159.

communist states of Eastern Europe illustrates how power, however concentrated and refined, cannot exist indefinitely without the charge of legitimation. East European dissidents in the 1970s, following the violent extinguishing of the Prague Spring in 1968, despaired of the grim effectiveness of one-party regimes that controlled the political system, the economy and the media and monitored the population in an intricate web of surveillance. Yet within 30 years, those same states had simply collapsed without, in most cases, a shot being fired.

It has always mattered what people thought, even though it may seem that only outward compliance counts. In the final years of the 19th century, the American neoclassical economist, John Bates Clark, developed a new theory of wages—the marginal productivity theory alluded to in the first chapter—that aimed to prove that "the natural effect of competition is … to give each producer the amount of wealth that he specifically brings into existence." This was a time when labour unrest was building and Henry George's *Progress and Poverty*- containing his ideas on the "enslavement of labor"—was one of the biggest selling books in America. Syndicalism was spreading, a militant form of trade unionism that aimed not for incremental improvements in workers' conditions but the root and branch replacement of the "wage system" with industrial democracy. Clark's concern was not that the apparatus of law and order was unequal to the task—the US had been subject to a huge and bitter strike wave in the closing years of the 19th century that had brought hundreds of deaths but been successfully suppressed—but that the capitalist system was losing legitimacy. The danger that the supposedly voluntary nature of the economic transaction might be widely exposed as a fraud had to be urgently countered:

> If they ["the laboring classes"] create a small amount of wealth and get the whole of it, they may not seek to revolutionize society; but if it were to appear that they produce an ample amount and get only a part of it, many of them would become revolutionaries and have every right to do so. The indictment that hangs over society is that of "exploiting labor." "Workmen" it is said, "are regularly robbed of their produce. This is done within the forms of the law, and by the natural working of competition." If this charge were proved, every right-minded man should become a socialist; and his zeal in transforming the industrial system would then measure and express his sense of justice.[43]

In the present era of a universal franchise and professed individual autonomy, the need to repackage obedience as meaningful consent is even more compelling. In such circumstances, Bookchin's notion of the "epistemology of rule" as possessing a dual nature—at once material and subjective— is extremely powerful. We live in societies characterised by an admixture of coercion and obedience. Under the banner of unfurling freedom, neoliberalism has executed draconian welfare conditionality policies, overseen huge rises in prison populations and guard labour, fought endless overseas wars

---

43  John Bates Clark, *The Distribution of Wealth: A Theory of Wages, Interest and Profits* (Macmillan, 1899), Chapter 1.

and placed myriad legal restrictions on labour union actions.[44] Its coercive side is undeniable. But, at the same time, the market system is a delicate flower. Intellectuals and politicians fret about capitalism's growing crisis of legitimacy. A right-wing journalist hammers out a warning that "the public is turning its back on the free market and re-embracing an atavistic version of socialism."[45] The former British Prime Minister felt obliged to defend the free market as "the greatest agent of collective human progress ever created" which has "led societies out of darkness and stagnation and into the light of the modern age."[46] Clearly building prisons is not enough.

Such anxiety is, I submit, rooted in the eternal vulnerability of hierarchy—the awareness that every day people literally create the world, construct anew its relationships, obligations and relations of command and obedience. And they could, just as easily, choose not to. Of course, states are immensely

---

44  In the United States, in 2011, there were 5.2 million "guard labourers," a category that comprises police officers, members of the armed forces, private security guards, prison and court officials, civilian employees of the military and weapons producers. There are as many private security guards as teachers. See Samuel Bowles and Arjun Jayadev, "One Nation Under Guard," New *York Times Opinionator*, 15 February, 2014.

45  Allister Heath, "There is sadly mass support for nationalisation and price controls," *City AM*, 5 November 2013.

46  Theresa May was speaking at an event to mark the 20th anniversary of the Bank of England's independence from political control. She repeated the claims at the Conservative party conference in October 2017.

physically powerful—there are consequences if people cease to faithfully follow the tramlines set out for them—but something essential is lost if people stop believing in the "correctness" of a system. Then obedience becomes compliance.

This brings to mind the distinction made by Hannah Arendt between power and violence. Although they are usually seen in combination, power and violence are not the same; in fact they are opposites. No government exclusively based on its capacity for violence has ever existed, said Arendt. They are all reliant, to a greater or lesser degree, on the support, or at least acquiescence of large sections of the governed. That is why, in revolutions, the vastly superior instruments of violence available to governments are not always decisive, and why the amassing by states of ever more awe-inspiring weaponry does not guarantee their invulnerability. Such invincibility depends on the power structure remaining operational—if commands are no longer obeyed and the army or police are not prepared to use their weapons, power drains away. This leaching of power is exactly what happened in Eastern Europe in 1989. "Everything depends on the power behind the violence," said Arendt. "The sudden dramatic breakdown of power that ushers in revolutions reveals in a flash how civil obedience—to laws, to rulers, to institutions—is but the outward manifestation of support and consent."[47] And what power craves, above all else, is legitimacy.

---

47  From "On Violence," in Hannah Arendt, *Crises of the Republic* (Mariner, 1972), 148. "Where commands are no longer obeyed," she writes, "the means of violence are of no use; and the question of this obedience is not decided by the command-obedience relation but by opinion and, of course, by the number of those who share it."

The obverse of this recognition is that we are all in some sense responsible. Not in the transparent blame-shifting way that asserts that corporations are merely neutral middle men connecting western consumers' insatiable desire for cheap goods with job hungry, dirt poor East Asians. So if workers in Dhaka slave in sweatshop conditions and die when unsafe buildings collapse on top of them, "we" are responsible because of our rapacious appetite for inexpensive clothes.[48] The mass of people do not sit atop this system, working its strings. But their participation is essential. This is what the late cultural critic Mark Fisher meant when he said that reclaiming political agency involves "accepting our insertion *at the level of desire* in the remorseless meat-grinder of Capital." We cannot just absolve ourselves by blaming evil or amoral élites. "What needs to be kept in mind," he asserted, "is *both* that capitalism is a hyper-abstract impersonal structure *and* that it would be nothing without our co-operation."[49]

---

48  This cart before horse logic asserts that corporations were prompted to relocate production in China, Bangladesh or Vietnam by consumer demand in the West. In reality the lure was massive hikes in profit because of infinitesimal labour costs. The technical term for this is "global labour arbitrage," defined by *The Economist* magazine as "taking advantage of lower wages abroad, especially in poor countries."

49  Mark Fisher, *Capitalist Realism* (Zero Books, 2009), 15.

## Non-Cooperation with Authority

Because, as Milgram showed, we can choose *not* to cooperate. Around one-third of the subjects in his obedience experiment defied authority, put their tools down, and refused to go on. But disobedience is not easy. It was the disobedient subjects, rather than their obedient equivalents, who experienced the burden of their actions. They pay, in Milgram's words, a considerable "psychic cost":

> The price of disobedience was a gnawing sense that one has been faithless. Even though he has chosen the morally correct action, the subject remains troubled by the disruption of the social order he has brought about, and cannot fully dispel the feeling that he deserted a cause to which he had pledged support.[50]

By contrast the ties that bind obedient subjects to their role are immensely robust. Not only do they fantasise about possible retribution from the experimenter if they rebel, they bridle at disturbing a social situation in which they are playing an essential part. "When the occasion is defined as one of hierarchy," said Milgram "any attempt to alter the defined structure will be experienced as a moral transgression and will evoke anxiety, shame, embarrassment and diminished feelings of self-worth."[51] Obedience—with all its attendant implications of inflicting possibly lethal electric shocks—

---

50  Milgram, *Obedience to Authority*, p 165.

51  Ibid., 153.

is perceived as a less painful alternative. Many obedient subjects undergo extreme inner discomfort—they sweat, they laugh hysterically or dig their fingernails into their skin—but they still obey. The strength of these feelings—the angst that rebellion constitutes a "moral transgression"—is an indication of how, in Bookchin's observation, class society organises "psychic structures" for command or obedience. Though it is not an instinctual relic of our animal evolution, the urge to obey displays a tenacity which is almost as strong.

But there were experimental conditions which eased the path for this moral transgression to happen. Of the numerous experimental variations dreamt up by Milgram, the most telling was the introduction of two actors, posing as subjects, who refuse to comply when ordered by the experimenter to shock the learner. Under this condition of peer rebellion, only one in ten real subjects goes on to deliver the highest electric shock, compared with nearly two-thirds in the basic experiment.

Part of the reason was the rebellious actors instil the idea of defying the experimenter—previously it might not have dawned on participants that this was possible. But much more was at play. With peer rebellion comes acceptance of rebellion as natural, as something valid because other people are doing it. In essence disobedience spreads because the moral transgression it entails that would normally serve to inhibit it is overpowered by conformity with the actions of a growing minority. Successful rebellion is rarely singular. "The revolt against malevolent authority is most effectively brought about by collective rather than individual action" noted Milgram. "This is a lesson every revolutionary group learns."

Not that rebellion is an ever-present possibility. There are times—long periods of stultifying conservatism—when individuals are so deeply submerged in their social roles that hierarchical systems are virtually frictionless and the meaning they impose on events is accepted without question. Eighteenth century England, Stalinism at its height, or 1950s America are examples of societies where discord was repressed by an overwhelming social purposefulness. However, there are also epochs when Milgram's agentic state—the willing suspension of a person's moral values so that they carry out another's wishes—causes visible strain and conflict. This is a sign of its weakness. Then, like a person in a light sleep, the obedient person can be woken up.

# Chapter Three

# The "Free" Labourer and the Eclipse of Scarcity

If a history of obedience is ever written, it would inescapably conclude that society has become strikingly *less* obedient. In 17th century England, for instance, the Biblical commandment to "honour thy father and thy mother" involved children habitually bowing before their parents. Parish priests instructed illiterate adolescents to behave "lowly and reverently" before their "betters" and servants and apprentices promised to obey their masters in all matters. When, in the heat of the English Revolution of the 1640s, Thomas Rainsborough claimed that the "poorest he that is in

England hath a life to live as the greatest he," his opponent, Henry Ireton, Oliver Cromwell's son-in-law, invoked the fifth commandment ("honour thy father and thy mother"), a law which he insisted "doth extend to all that are our governors."[1]

Plato in *The Republic*, the foundation text of western political thought, recommended tales of eternal punishment in the afterlife as a way of keeping the multitude in line. Fear of the Last Judgement as a restraint on the rebelliousness and disobedience of the masses has played a palpable role in history, only abating in the last 150 years or so. Until at least the middle of the 19th century English courts regarded oaths by people who didn't believe in a "future state" as worthless because fear of hell wouldn't prevent them lying.[2]

These were forms of obedience rather than coercion because they involved the inner beliefs—and through this the outward behaviour—of the oppressed. Their power lay in how effectively they were internalised. However, they have all faded as a means of control—few people consciously obey their "betters" or act morally in this life because they fear eternal suffering in the next.

However, amidst this dilution of obedience, one form has flourished rather than disappeared. That form is wage labour—the agreement to obey in return for the gift of wages, the means of living. In the last forty years, wage labour has been reinvigorated as a moral obligation, without which a person is nothing but a drain on resources. But behind

---

1   Peter Laslett, *The World We Have Lost—Further Explored* (Routledge, 2000), 20, 217-219.

2   John Stuart Mill, *On Liberty* (Penguin Classics, 1987), 91.

this ethical exhortation is the conviction that a modern, interdependent, productive economy is reliant on mass wage labour. We cannot do without this form of obedience even if we wanted to.

As the 21st century progresses, it is this underlying justification of wage labour that is coming under scrutiny. But to understand how the ground is shifting beneath the wage system, it is necessary to examine the fate of older forms of mass labour, once thought indispensable.

## Capitalism and Slavery

In late 18th century Britain, the slave trade and West Indian slavery, through the mass production of sugar they enabled, were regarded as essential props of national prosperity. In *Capitalism and Slavery*, the young West Indian academic and the future Prime Minister of Trinidad and Tobago, Eric Williams, demonstrated how profits from the triangular trade "fertilized the entire productive system" of Great Britain.[3] Capital from slavery helped finance James Watts' steam engine, some of the first railway projects and several ironworks.[4] The anti-slavery movement was initially widely

---

3   Eric Williams, *Capitalism and Slavery* (University of North Carolina Press, 1944), 105.

4   Aside from industrial development, Williams emphasised the importance of the slave trade to the growth of banking and insurance—in particular, to household names such as Barclays (estimated now to be the largest corporate shareholder in the world) and Lloyd's.

hated (that is, not just by West Indian plantation owners) because, in exposing the torments that lay behind the slave trade, it was regarded as endangering the source of British wealth.

But following the spectacular progress of the Industrial Revolution and the growth of domestic wage labour, West Indian slavery and the monopoly on sugar imports it entailed, diminished in importance, eventually being perceived as an impediment to wealth rather than an enhancement of it. It was then that the moral case of the abolitionists, now aligned with material self-interest, could gain traction. Much as Britain came to proselytize for free trade whereas its prior industrial development depended on tariffs, monopolies and the destruction of manufacturing in the colonies, it could now afford to evangelise against the monstrosity of slavery. "Even the great mass movements, and the anti-slavery mass movement was one of the greatest of these," said Williams, "show a curious affinity with the rise and development of new interests and the necessity of the destruction of the old."[5]

Extrapolating from Williams, one can discern a principle. Immense suffering—and the slave trade certainly fits that description—is not widely perceived in its true light until it is also perceived as unnecessary, or at least inessential. Aristotle, for example, considered one of the most insightful philosophers in history, never questioned the morality of slavery or the natural right of male Athenians to rule over all other peoples, even though he himself wasn't Athenian. In the ancient world, slavery was considered an immutable part

---

5    Williams, *Capitalism and Slavery*, 211.

of life. The humanitarian landmarks of the 19th century—the abolition of the British slave trade in 1807, the dissolution of slavery in the British Empire in 1834, the ending of slavery in the US in 1865 and the emancipation of the Russian serfs four years earlier—were not chimeras. But they were accompanied by the growing realisation that, in the midst of the immense technological transformation of the first Industrial Revolution, maintaining "a permanent labour force at an employer's expense, especially when demand was seasonal or subject to frequent market fluctuations," was economically irrational.[6] Wage labour, by contrast, made more economic sense because it involved utilising a *temporary* labour force. Besieged supporters of chattel slavery even asserted that theirs was a morally superior system because slave-owners had an interest in looking after their property at all times rather than using workers when necessary and then casting them aside.

What doomed chattel slavery and serfdom in the 19th century was not only a broadening of ethical scope, but the exponential growth of labour productivity and the wage labour system. The wage system brought in its train terrible humanitarian abuses—the employment of children, overwork, infectious diseases, malnutrition, unsanitary conditions and hugely overcrowded housing. But apart from the rising socialist movement, few suggested abolishing the wage system altogether. It was deemed too essential to modern life for such radical surgery to be countenanced. Rather, its

---

6    See Harry Shutt, "The End of Wage Slavery," *Harryshutt.com*, 8 April, 2018.

excesses had to be ameliorated. Karl Polanyi's "protective countermovement" swung into action—legislation restricted the employment of children, limited working hours, introduced compulsory education and grudgingly permitted trade unions to operate.[7] This was the mirror opposite of what happened to chattel slavery. There were attempts in the early 19th century to ameliorate conditions for slaves. In 1823 the British government proposed reforms to slavery in the West Indies—a nine-hour day, the abolition of the whip and the appointment of a "Protector of Slaves." But the attempts failed—the thing itself was the problem and its days were numbered.

Wage labour, by contrast, being viewed as the engine of progress and the essential factor behind increasing wealth, was rationalised as the pinnacle of freedom. Under capitalism, the putatively voluntary nature of contracts between legal equals meant that the labourer was "free," not enslaved. The economic liberals, as seen in Chapter 1, protested with all of their might that wage labour was the utter antithesis of slavery and serfdom—it involved "cooperation" or "coordination" of individual efforts, but never brute submission to an employer's will. The wage system thus became obedience hidden in plain sight. It was left to rebels and revolutionaries to state the inconvenient reality. "Is there a workshop where obedience is

---

7   Karl Polanyi, *The Great Transformation* (Beacon Press, 1944), 151. Polanyi emphasises that the individuals behind these legislative restraints on the wage labour system "were as a rule uncompromising opponents of socialism, or any other form of collectivism."

not demanded—not to the difficulties or qualities of the labor to be performed—but to the caprice of he who pays the wages of his servants?" asked an anonymous writer in the journal of the American Knights of Labor, which organised both black and white workers, in 1885.[8]

What gave strength to these ideological rationalisations was that the signature organisation of the maturing capitalist system—the corporation (initially known as the joint-stock company)—relied on a system of command and control, a division of labour, the precise articulation of tasks and unquestioning obedience.

To the sociologist Max Weber, like Stanley Milgram fascinated by the nature of obedience, the corporation was the ideal and "rational" economic organisation of the age. It was organised as a pyramid, with decisions flowing from the top down. Senior managers reported to a governing board of directors, while workers at various levels of the organisation obeyed precise instructions from above. Inside the corporation there was a career structure with promotion conditional on the appraisal of superiors.[9]

As chattel slavery and serfdom slipped from the stage of history, the "essential superstructure of the capitalist

---

8    Quoted in Alex Gourevitch, "Wage-Slavery and Republican Liberty," *Jacobin*, February 2013.

9    Milgram, too, thought that promotion was essential for a hierarchical organisation. "'The 'promotion' carries with it profound emotional gratification for the individual but its special feature is the fact that it ensures the continuity of hierarchical form," Milgram, *Obedience to Authority*, 139.

economy" was put in place across Western economies.[10] Beginning in the 1850s, stock exchanges allowed the public trading of shares in corporations and their expansion through outside investment. Limited liability—the provision that the investor-owner, should things go wrong, is only liable for the sum total of his/her investment, not their share of the entire debts of the company—encouraged the formation and multiplication of capital. This permitted a dynamism and productiveness profoundly different from traditional forms of economic activity.

The giant, vertically integrated corporation—attracting capital investment from outside to finance its operations and separating its workforce from any ownership or control over the means of production—became the dominant economic form across the world. This has culminated in the situation today where the top 500 globally traded companies have a combined revenue equivalent to one third of world GDP.[11] Regardless of whether economic entities are literally corporations (that is to say that the public can buy shares in them and they are not privately owned by individuals), the internal corporate form has become the template for economic organisation per se.

This is so despite the fact that the corporation is supremely autocratic. A "corporation or an industry is, if we were to think of it in political terms, fascist," said Noam Chomsky

---

10  See Harry Shutt, "The Withering Away of the Financial Industry," *Harryshutt.com*, 8 April, 2015.

11  Quoted in Jeremy Rifkin, The Zero Marginal Cost Society (Palgrave Macmillan, 2014), 67.

in 1973, "that is, it has tight control at the top and strict obedience has to be established at every level—there's a little bargaining, a little give and take, but the line of authority is perfectly straightforward."[12] Max Weber explicitly admitted that the voluntary nature of obedience embodied by the corporation was reliant on the existence of a property-less mass of potential wage labourers forced to rent themselves out "under the compulsion of the whip of hunger."[13]

Thus, again we confront the ambiguous nature of obedience. It is not the same as coercion. The obedient person feels a moral obligation to obey, not merely fear of the consequences if they defy orders. Yet the conditions leading up to the enactment of obedience are invariably anything but free. For example, the obedience embodied in corporations has a subjective basis in previous class relations, such as the medieval Great Chain of Being, which crystallised obedience to the wishes of people of higher status as natural and God given. Everyone—serfs, servants, yeomen, knights, lords and even monarchs—had a place within the hierarchy because "God hath placed them there" and social harmony depended on them faithfully performing their duties and obeying those above them.[14] Yet objectively capitalist obedience was also dependent on the European enclosures from the 16th century onwards which forcibly uprooted peasants

---

12  Interview with Noam Chomsky, "One Man's View," *Business Today*, May 1973.

13  Quoted in Randall Collins, "Weber's Last Theory of Capitalism," *American Sociological Review*, Vol 45, No. 6, December 1980, 928.

14  Peter Laslett, *The World We Have Lost*, 20.

from common lands, creating millions of putatively "free" labourers with little choice but to hire themselves out in the mills and factories. The same dualism—between ostensible consent and practical compulsion deriving from economic vulnerability—defines capitalism today.

In the last century, the face of the system began to change. The economies of scale and huge rises in productivity that the corporation engendered produced great wealth which, in time and under the conditions of a managed capitalism, began to seep into wider society. Thomas Piketty has described the emergence of a "patrimonial" (i.e. property-owning) middle class in the 20th century as an "important, if fragile, historical innovation". Comprising roughly 40 per cent of the population in Europe and the U.S., this group has managed to lay its hands on merely a "few crumbs" of the great wealth of society—between one third and one quarter.[15] Nevertheless, they are far from destitute and have much more to lose than their chains. Hence, the justification of corporate capitalism has increasingly taken a utilitarian form. The extremely shaky argument that shareholder investors—as opposed to a corporation's workforce—deserve sole ownership of the wealth generated by society (the "neo-classical" argument) has been superseded by the pragmatic contention that capitalism, despite the great inequalities of wealth and power it entails, is more efficient than any conceivable alternative and increases the wealth and general welfare of society. In Weberian terms, society at large has an interest in obedience

---

15  Thomas Piketty, *Capital in the Twenty-First Century* (Harvard University Press, 2014), 261-262.

because through obedience—in the form of universal wage labour—we enjoy wealth undreamed of by past generations.

## The Future We Never Had

But the idea that the wage system would, one day, outlive its usefulness never entirely went away. In 1930, the British economist, John Maynard Keynes, wrote a short 12-page essay called *Economic Possibilities for our Grandchildren.*[16] Virtually ignored at the time, the essay has enjoyed a remarkable second life because of Keynes' prediction that in 100 years' time—i.e. 2030—technological advancement would mean people would regularly be working 3 hour days or 15 hour weeks. Keynes was as far from an idle dreamer as it is possible to be—a hard-headed economist, he invested millions on the stock market as bursar of King's College, Cambridge. Yet he was soberly asserting that the 21st century progeny of '30s toilers—"us" in other words—would be free to discard "distasteful and unjust" economic rewards and penalties, because they were no longer necessary. The human race would emerge from "the tunnel of economic necessity" into a new world where the most pressing concern will be how to occupy one's leisure time. In the words of two modern-day admirers, Keynes believed that capitalism would "abolish itself when its work was done."[17]

---

16  All subsequent quotes are taken from John Maynard Keynes, *Essays in Persuasion* (Palgrave Macmillan, 2010), 321-332.

17  Robert Skidelsky and Edward Skidelsky, *How Much is Enough? Money and the good life* (The Other Press, 2012), 6.

As is now quite apparent, no such voluntary euthanasia on the part of the capitalist system is going to happen. The reason can be found in Keynes' original explanation for surges in the "standard of life": technological improvement—such as steam, coal, electricity, steel, and mass production—allied to the *accumulation of capital.* The latter—money invested to make more money which is then invested again and so on ad infinitum—drives the process and is the beating heart of the capitalist system. Keynes gave the example of Queen Elizabeth I of England who was a shareholder in Francis Drake's privateering *Golden Hind* expedition of 1577. Drake circumnavigated the globe and, in one incident, captured a Spanish galleon which held treasure worth (in today's money) £480 million. The profits from Drake's expedition were invested in the Levant Company (to secure trading rights with the Ottoman Empire). And from the profits of the Levant Company, the East India Company was founded, "the foundation," in Keynes' words, "of England's subsequent foreign investment."[18]

Once set in motion, capital accumulation does not stop. The reason why Keynes' belief that in the 21st century we would have the breathing space to devote "our further energies to non-economic purposes" and "value ends over means" has not come to pass is that this process of accumulating capital has not abated; it still determines the nature of economic activity. Keynes thought the rate of capital accumulation would be limited by the absence of war, population control and scientific authority. However, as we are now painfully

---

18  Keynes, *Essays in Persuasion*, 324.

aware, capital accumulation has an imperative and logic of its own, to which other social needs, such as the preservation of a liveable climate or the wish to pursue life's "non-economic purposes," are sacrificed.

*Capital-ism* involves the advancing of money to make more money, the generation (hopefully from the point of view of the capitalist) of a financial return that is invested again, barring some deductions for luxury consumption. "Without that expansion there can be no capital. A zero-growth capitalist economy is a logical and exclusionary contradiction. It simply cannot exist," writes geographer David Harvey.[19] Harvey, like Keynes in 1930, highlights the underrated power of compound interest which entails adding interest to the interest previously accumulated. However, unlike Keynes, Harvey does not imagine that capital accumulation will simply wither away when the time is right. He posits a "satisfactory" growth rate of 3 per cent a year, enough to give capitalists a positive return on their investment. This necessitates, he says, "finding profitable investment opportunities for an extra nearly $2 trillion compared to the "mere" $6 billion that was needed in 1970. By the time 2030 rolls around, when estimates suggest the global economy should be more than $96 trillion, profitable investment opportunities of close to $3 trillion will be needed."[20]

---

19  David Harvey, *Seventeen Contradictions and the End of Capitalism* (Profile Books, 2014), 232.

20  Ibid. In the US, the Eurozone and the UK, growth has not attained the 3 per cent benchmark since before the financial crisis over a

Wage labour is intimately tied to the accumulation of capital and its endless search for "profitable opportunities." It entails the obligation of those without wealth to temporarily rent themselves to the owners of resources in order to add

---

decade ago. The consequences in a free market economy would be huge losses and bankruptcies. However, we do not live in a free market economy. Governments responded to the 2008 financial crisis by massive bail-outs (worth $7.7 trillion and $1.5 trillion in the UK), followed by concerted attempts to artificially boost the value of financial assets such as equities, a technique known by the neutral sounding name of Quantitative Easing (QE). The level of money creation through QE has been enormous—the US spent $4.5 trillion (the equivalent of giving $56,000 to every American citizen), the UK £475 billion and the European Central Bank up to €80 billion a month. Japan, the nation which invented QE in the 1990s, upped the ante even further in 2013 with Qualitative and Quantitative Easing (QQE), a monetary easing programme so huge (£1.8 trillion) it had to be given a different name. In total, maybe 20 per cent of world GDP consists of fiat (invented) money. Under QE the central bank (e.g. the Federal Reserve or the Bank of England) buys government bonds from banks, which then have low cost funds to invest. QE lowers the interest rate by decreasing the yield on government bonds which pay fixed interest. As a result, investors are "incentivised" to switch their funds into other assets such as the stock market or property. The result has been artificially generated stock market booms—a "natural" stock market boom would anticipate higher profitability among companies—amidst insipid economic growth. The prime beneficiaries have been banks and other owners of financial assets.

value to economic activities in return for which they are given the material means of life.[21] Therefore this obligation will not disappear while capitalism remains in existence. And capitalism, like a perpetual motion machine, is not about to abolish itself.

## Capitalism Negates Itself

This became the Marxist dilemma, once the hope that capitalism would generate its own "gravediggers" proved illusory.[22] Contrary to myth, Marxian economics, though it regards capitalism as inherently unstable, does not predict an inevitable capitalist apocalypse. Marx's analysis was cyclical. His "fundamental law of capitalism" was that, subject to certain counter-tendencies, the rate of profit would decline, eventually precipitating an economic crisis. Competition compels capitalists to automate and replace workers with machines. This temporarily increases profit but as, according to Marx, human labour is the ultimate source of profit, the average rate of profit in the economy as a whole contracts as the "organic composition of capital"—the share taken up by machinery and technology as opposed to labour power—

---

21  The pool of people requiring wage labour to survive is enormous even in putatively rich countries. In the UK, the fifth largest economy in the world, more than 16 million people have less than £100 in savings. Brian Milligan, "Millions have less than £100 in savings, study finds," *BBC News*, 29 September 2016.

22  Karl Marx and Friedrich Engels, *The Communist Manifesto* (Oxford World's Classics, 1992), 16.

rises. If the counter-tendencies—such as new markets, or new sources of cheap labour—can't fill the gap, recession results. But, importantly, this is not a terminal problem. Once the slump has played itself out—and capital value is destroyed—the whole "crap," in his description, can begin again.

However, a new school of thought argues that the inescapable competitive process at the heart of the Marxist analysis—increasing mechanisation which excludes labour from the production process generating rising productivity—is now not leading merely to the decline of profit but its elimination.[23] This is because the "dynamism of competitive markets" produces an inherent drive to reduce marginal costs—the cost of producing extra copies of a given product.[24] We are now at the stage where, in many sectors of the economy, it costs nothing or nearly nothing to produce additional goods—so-called "zero marginal costs." At first glance, as with the Marxist compulsion to automate and reduce the inputs of human labour, this might appear an unadulterated boon from the point of view of the capitalist—labour costs shrink to oblivion and profits snowball. However, as rival firms also cross the threshold of zero marginal costs, competitive pressures force prices downwards. The economy conforms to, in the words of former US Treasury Secretary,

---

23  This "school" includes the subsequently quoted Jeremy Rifkin, but also leftist journalist and broadcaster Paul Mason who asserts that "an economy based on information, with its tendency to zero-cost products and weak property rights, cannot be a capitalist economy." (Paul Mason, *PostCapitalism* (Allen Lane, 2015), 126.

24  Rifkin, *Zero Marginal Cost Society*, 9.

Larry Summers, "one of the most fundamental principles of economics"—that prices equal marginal costs.[25] "But if consumers pay only for the marginal costs and those costs continue to race toward zero," says American social theorist Jeremy Rifkin, "businesses would not be able to ensure a return on their investment and sufficient profit to satisfy their shareholders":

> When marginal costs shrink to near zero, profit disappears because goods and services have been liberated from market pricing. They become essentially free. When most things become nearly free, the whole operating rationale of capitalism as an organizing mechanism to produce and distribute goods and services becomes meaningless. That's because capitalism's dynamism feeds off scarcity. If resources, goods and services are scarce, they have exchange value and can be priced in the marketplace beyond what they cost to bring them there. But when the marginal cost of producing those goods and services approaches zero and the price becomes nearly free, the capitalist system loses its hold over scarcity and the ability to profit from another's dependency.[26]

The "zero marginal cost society" contradicts the notion that wage labour is essential to a modern, productive, consuming economy. In fact, this economy is superabundantly

---

25  See J. Bradford DeLong and Lawrence H. Summers, "The 'New Economy': Background, Historical Perspective, Questions and Speculations" (Federal Reserve Bank of Kansas, 2001), 35.

26  Rifkin, *Zero Marginal Cost Society*, 9, 333.

productive because there is minimal human input into the production process. Manufacturing techniques such as 3D Printing are enabling the immediate production of an infinite variety of customised physical objects at minimal cost and without human labour. Also known as additive manufacturing, 3D Printing involves the building up of a physical product, layer by layer, inside a printer using inputs such as molten plastic or molten metal. The type of products which can be produced by 3D Printing is growing by the year and now includes small homes, cars, jewellery, aeroplane parts and even artificial human tissue. The process been compared to the replicator in the *Star Trek* television series—a machine that can be programmed to produce virtually any desired object. The 3D printing "factory" can be located in homes or neighbourhoods and does not require the existence of a centralised factory or the transport of goods, frequently now across oceans, from factory to shop. It is indicative of forms of technology that, rather than fuelling the model of wage earner and consumer capitalism as they have for the last 150 years, are negating it and rendering it redundant.

Indeed, wage labour, claim numerous theorists, is being automated out of existence by the very force that created it in the first place—capitalist competition. Intelligent technology, says Rifkin, is replacing not only mass manufacturing jobs but the work of salaried professionals as well. "Computers are being programmed to recognise patterns, advance hypotheses, implement solutions and even decipher communication and translate complex metaphors from one language to another in real time."[27] Thus automation—basically Artificial Intelligence plus computerisation—is now threatening to not only cut another swathe through the remaining stock of manual jobs but for the first time eat into the mainstays of middle class employment, or what has been dubbed "communicative labour."[28] Middle managers, accountants, marketers and graphic designers are all ripe for displacement by machines employers don't have to pay. Sociologist Randall Collins predicts the rise of advanced robots endowed with sensors and on-board computers ready to take over middle class skilled work "and then displace managers and expert professionals." He envisages 50 to 70% unemployment by the middle of this century and a deep structural capitalist crisis.[29]

Taking a birds-eye perspective on the history of capitalism, a trajectory can be detected. The First Industrial Revolution (steam power, machine tools etc. from the late 18th century onwards)—the phenomenon analysed by Eric Williams in *Capitalism and Slavery*—put paid to slave and serf labour. The Second Industrial Revolution—electricity, assembly lines, steel production, chemicals—destroyed agriculture as a source of employment. The Information Technology revolution of the 1980s and '90s facilitated globalisation and the rise of finance, laying waste to large tranches of manufacturing industry in western countries. The Third

---

27  Ibid., 157.

28  Randall Collins, "The End of Middle Class Work: No More
    Escapes," in Randall Collins et al., *Does Capitalism Have a Future?*
    (Oxford University Press, 2013), 40.

29  Ibid.

Industrial Revolution—computerisation and intelligent technology—is set to decimate the remaining bastions of wage labour, displacing the communicative functions of salaried professionals and managers.

But, after this happens, all the relations of control that capitalism inherited from the past and innovated itself, will be exhausted. Either humanity scraps over the residual jobs servicing the élite and plunges into a new dark age of conflict and repression or it enters a new era. Rifkin, optimistically, assumes the latter. Millions of "prosumers" (producers and consumers combined) will take advantage of the new economic paradigm to share information, renewable energy and 3D printed products. They will become connected to the "Internet of Things," driving efficiencies and the marginal cost of progressively more and more products and services towards zero, although he neglects say how these "prosumers" will procure the income to survive.

From a seemingly invincible way of organising economic and social life, capitalism—and its attendant social relations personified by the giant corporation—will shrink to a niche sector of the economy. "The condition for capital is wage labour," said Marx and Engels.[30] But that condition, says Rifkin, will no longer exist:

> A half century from now, our grandchildren are likely to look back on the era of mass employment in the market with the same sense of utter disbelief as we look upon slavery and serfdom in former times. The very idea that a human

---

30  Marx and Engels, *The Communist Manifesto*, 15.

being's worth was measured almost exclusively by his or her productive output of goods and services will seem primitive, even barbaric, and be regarded as a terrible loss of human value to our progeny living in a highly automated world.[31]

Thus, ironically, capitalism and wage labour will not be undone by the opposition and hostility they provoke. The culprit will be something the system cannot overcome or co-opt—its own inherent technological inventiveness.

## O Robot Where Art Thou?

However, there is something amiss with the chronology presented above. In the first and second industrial revolutions, technology and capitalism advanced cheek to cheek. Technological innovations such as James Watt's steam engine or Henry Ford's assembly line were instantly utilized in the service of profit. As a result, productivity spiralled and the wealth of society increased. As electricity steadily replaced steam power in factories, for example, there was a 300 per cent increase in productivity. This is how capitalism gained its reputation. The "constant revolutionizing of production, uninterrupted disturbance of all social conditions, everlasting uncertainty and agitation," wrote Marx and Engels in *The Communist Manifesto*, "distinguish the bourgeois epoch from all earlier ones."[32]

---

31  Rifkin, *Zero Marginal Cost Society*, 161-162. Our grandchildren would of course be Keynes' great-great-grandchildren.

32  Marx and Engels, *Communist Manifesto*, 6.

A century later, the "bourgeois epoch" seemed to have lost none of its revolutionary élan. The Austrian-American economist Joseph Schumpeter—writing from an avowedly pro-capitalist perspective—could laud the role of the entrepreneur and innovator in imbuing capitalism with a dynamism that unmistakably distinguished it from all previous ages. He famously referred to the "gale of creative destruction ... that incessantly revolutionizes the economic structure from within, incessantly destroying the old one and incessantly creating a new one."[33] Marx regarded capitalism as oppressive, immiserating and dehumanizing but, in the final analysis, progressive because the technological leaps it entailed paved the way for a rational, socialist society. The "Schumpeterians," by contrast, even though the concept of creative destruction seemed to be derived from Marx, "gloried in capitalism's endless creativity while treating the destructiveness as mostly a matter of the normal costs of doing business."[34] Nonetheless both anti-capitalist and pro-capitalist concurred that capitalism, as an economic and social system, was astoundingly creative.

However, that was then. Notwithstanding the chorus of voices heralding the earth-shattering implications of the Third Industrial Revolution, the gale of creative destruction seems to have given way to an oppressive stillness. Were the digital/robot revolution to be merrily scything through the analogue

---

33  The phrase is from Joseph Schumpeter's 1942 book, *Capitalism, Socialism and Democracy*.

34  David Harvey, *The Enigma of Capital and the Crises of Capitalism* (Profile Books, 2011), 46.

economy, this would show up in soaring productivity figures, which measure output per worker; in effect a proxy for how efficiently the economy uses labour, capital and available technologies. "Extreme productivity" would become the norm as the economy approached zero marginal costs, and both production and labour costs shrank towards oblivion.[35] However, the opposite is the case. Economists scratch their heads over the "productivity puzzle"—the paradox that profitability seems to have recovered following the 2008-9 crash but productivity remains in the doldrums. According to the International Monetary Fund, productivity in the "advanced" economies has shrunk to an annual rate of just 0.3 per cent, compared to an average of 1 per cent before the crisis a decade before. But even prior to the Great Financial Crisis, productivity was slowing and pales in comparison with the 5 per cent regularly achieved in the period from 1948 to 1973. Christine Lagarde, managing director of the IMF, poses the anomaly of "technological breakthroughs everywhere *except* in the productivity statistics"—a sure sign that, in a complete reversal of the pattern of capitalist history, technological innovations are *not* being put to use in the economy.[36]

This uncreative inertia is evident in other ways too. The level of business investment—the financing of new equipment, machinery or IT which would naturally rise if new technologies were being readied for use—has fallen to

---

35  The phrase is Rifkin's. See Rifkin, *Zero Marginal Cost Society*, 85.

36  See Christine Lagarde, "Reinvigorating Productivity Growth," Speech for the International Monetary Fund, 3 April, 2017.

historic lows. According to the United Nations Conference on Trade and Development, the share of GDP taken up by "fixed capital formation" in the leading capitalist countries (France, Germany, the UK, Japan and the United States), fell from 20 per cent in 1980 to 14 per cent in 2015.[37] Studies indicate that the largest area of job growth has been in low paying service jobs which are difficult to automate; a trend encouraged by the policy of tax credits, in countries like the US and UK, which subsidise low wage work.

In fact, the evidence is that wage labour is not being automated out of existence—there are more jobs in Euro-American countries than there were thirty years ago. However, labour is undergoing another transformation. In the 19th century, slavery and serfdom were replaced by wage labour because, in part, the latter was more economically efficient. Wage labour, in contrast to chattel slavery, only required the employer to take responsibility for their workforce while they were at work. The fastest areas of job growth now are self-employment and "tasking"—payment for discrete tasks such as fast food delivery, domestic jobs, taxi services, dog

---

37  See Chart 5.2, "Corporate Profits and Investment, 1980-2015" in *The United Nations Conference on Trade and Development, Trade and Development Report 2016*, 143. Figures specifically about the US—though evidently using a different means of calculation— show a similar fall. According to statistics from the Bureau of Economic Analysis, "private non-residential fixed investment" as a share of GDP dropped from 3.8% in the 1980s to 2.4% in the first decade of the 21st century.

walking, and the like.[38] From the perspective of the profit-seeking entrepreneur the advantage of these new forms of "on-demand" labour is that they require even less financial responsibility than traditional wage labour—no obligation for holiday or sick pay, for example. Tools and work clothes also have to be supplied by the "tasker." The nature of the obedience inculcated by these new forms of work is probably less onerous than with traditional office and factory jobs. But the tasker's role is still to add value, often to a greater degree than in the past. So-called labour brokers, who put sellers of servicers in touch with buyers, can take a cut of 20 per cent or more from transactions.[39] Thus, workers are both freer and more exploited.

## The Myth of Competitive Capitalism

Taken together, these trends indicate that the basic assumption of those who predict the inevitable trajectory of capitalism towards zero marginal costs—that "the dynamism of competitive markets" makes such a destination inescapable—is mistaken. Capitalism is still driven by the all-encompassing need to maximise profit, but no longer by competition. Ironically, perhaps, this premise—that competition drives automation and increases in productivity—is at root impeccably Marxist. However, as David Graeber has argued, the conviction that capitalism "is in its nature technologically progressive" is a 19th century anachronism:

38  Guy Standing, *The Corruption of Capitalism* (Biteback
    Publishing, 2016), Chapter 6.

39  Ibid, 213.

It would seem that Marx and Engels, in their giddy enthusiasm for the industrial revolutions of their day, were simply wrong about this. Or to be more precise: they were right to insist that the mechanization of industrial production would eventually destroy capitalism; they were wrong to predict that market competition would compel factory owners to go on with mechanization anyway. If it didn't happen, it can only be because market competition is not, in fact, as essential to the nature of capitalism as they had assumed.[40]

But it wasn't only Karl Marx who viewed market competition and capitalism as synonymous. Mainstream business theory regards monopolies as temporary aberrations that allow dominant firms to fend off competitors and thus block innovations that, had they been allowed to proceed, would have increased productivity and reduced the prices of goods to consumers. The assumption is that, under a "market system," perfect competition is the normal state of affairs. Under such "natural" conditions, the sheer number of firms means that one individual company—or group of companies— cannot determine the level of prices. They are equally subject to uncontrollable "market forces." In such an innately competitive economy, the drift to near zero marginal costs is a real threat. Companies, should they be aware of it, may not like the eventual destination (the end of profit) but they are powerless to do anything about it. Competition ordains that it will happen, that the economy aligns with the basic principle that prices to consumers equal marginal production costs.

---

40  David Graeber, *The Utopia of Rules* (Melville House, 2015), 143.

The reality, however, is very different from this textbook version of capitalism. Since the 1960s, a branch of left-wing economic thought has understood that the era of the truly competitive capitalist economy—in which numerous firms battle for market share leading to the bankruptcy of many participants—is a thing of the past. It has been superseded by "monopoly capitalism" in which a small number of very large companies are able to determine investment, output, pricing and profit levels in the economy and thwart new entrants from usurping their position.[41] They are even in a position to

---

41 There is a clear schism in Marxian economics between adherents of the theory of monopoly capitalism and those who still hold to Marx's belief that the ultimate cause of crises is an economy-wide decline in the rate of profit. The monopoly capital school of thought, by contrast, believe that, under conditions of monopoly and oligopoly, the rate of surplus extracted by large corporations continues to rise, leading to stagnation because the resultant level of production cannot be absorbed by consumers. It was generally held in economics that Marx's contention of a decline in the rate of profit had been disproved by real-world conditions. However, Marxian economists, such as Michael Roberts and Andrew Kliman, claim that this is simply mistaken and that a decline in the rate of profit—defined as the amount of profit received as a proportion of capital originally advanced—is the ultimate cause of economic downturns such as the Great Depression and the Great Financial Crisis. If they are correct then capitalism must still retain a significant element of competitiveness—for the tendency of the decline in the rate of profit to work its way through the economy—despite the undoubted empirical fact that it has become far more concentrated, and thus less competitive, than in the

suppress or delay the introduction of new technologies if these conflict with their profit maximisation strategies. Momentous innovations, such as the steam engine or the motor car, thus become less likely in an era of monopoly capitalism.[42]

The trend towards greater concentration—and thus less competition—in the business sector has hugely accelerated in recent years. There has been a frenzy of mergers and acquisitions—escalated by the crisis of 2008-9—from which has emerged progressively larger economic entities with greater market share and power to shape the wider economic and political climate. In 2016, *The Economist* magazine analysed 900 sectors of the US economy and found that 2/3rds became more concentrated between 1997 and 2012.[43] As a

---

past. Perhaps the key to this riddle is the slowing of automation. Greater mechanization is an integral part of the decline in the rate of profit—as machinery gradually displaces human labour (the source of profit), the profit rate slumps. But as productivity and automation have stalled in recent decades, maybe the decline in the rate of profit has been similarly curtailed.

42  For the monopoly capital thesis, see John Bellamy Foster and Robert W. McChesney, *The Endless Crisis: How Monopoly-Finance Capital Produces Stagnation and Upheaval from the USA to China* (Monthly Review Press, 2012). The internet and digital communication may seem to contradict the anti-innovation thesis but these were developed outside the private sector (the state/NGOs) and the world-wide-web was unpatented. In addition, it took some years before their usefulness was realised by the corporate sector.

43  "Too much of a good thing," *The Economist*, 26 March 2016.

result, corporate America was raking in "exceptional profits" of about $300 billion a year, equivalent to a third of taxed operating profits. And contrary to "one of the fundamental principles of economics"—that prices equal marginal costs— these profits were *not* being passed on to the consumer, with some more concentrated sectors of the economy, according to *The Economist*'s analysis, seeing price rises of double the rate of inflation.

Orthodox economic theory, wedded to a conception of perfect competition, has never been able to transcend its 19th century origins. In this world, impersonal price competition lies at the heart of a "self-regulating" market guided by Adam Smith's invisible hand. In reality, however, in conditions of monopoly and oligopoly, the way corporations set themselves apart is not primarily through the objective measure of market pricing but through how their products are subjectively perceived—advertising and branding. These techniques have now reached such a level of saturation—to the degree that it is hard for any sentient being on the planet to avoid their reach—that it is easy to overlook their economic utility. But the function of branding, aside from increasing market share and building customer loyalty, is that it allows brand-owners "to charge more for their products than a simple mark-up over cost."[44]

What all this means is that there is no such thing anymore as pure market pricing. Many more elements contribute to the pricing of products than the simple cost of producing them. Thus, the logic of theorists like Jeremy Rifkin—that near zero

---

44  Ibid.

marginal costs will destroy profit because goods and services will be "liberated from market pricing"—does not hold true. This is not to deny the possibility or even actuality of near zero production costs. However, the defence mechanisms of contemporary capitalism against their approach—branding, licensing and monopoly—are strong. In all likelihood should zero marginal costs become widely adopted under this economic system, they will immeasurably boost price mark-ups, profits and thus the wealth of the top 0.01 per cent. Inequality, already more extreme than at any other time in history, will rise beyond all comprehension.

Nor is there a simple parallel between the eclipse of chattel slavery and serfdom in the 19th century by the wage system, and the future of wage labour now. These older forms of domination were usurped by an intensely competitive form of capitalism that was vastly more productive than any previous economic order. The vested interests in favour of their preservation were also confronted with equally wealthy and powerful proponents of change, who could see the wealth-creating effects of capital unfolding before their eyes. Today, we are in the grip of a "mature" system, whose loyal adherents in the corridors of power do not care how economically superfluous it becomes. Only that it is preserved.

## Post-Scarcity, Post-Capitalism

Virtually since its inception capitalism has been plagued by its own shadow. Anti-capitalism, in this sense, is not just visceral hostility but a realisation that capitalism, by virtue of its immense productivity compared with previous economic orders, makes possible its own negation—a technologically advanced, automated society shorn of relations of control and obedience. Marx famously distinguished between the "realm of necessity" and the "realm of freedom," the latter allowing the development of human energy "as an end in itself" and resting on a fall in working hours. Oscar Wilde looked forward to a future time when humanity occupied itself with "making beautiful things, or reading beautiful things, or simply contemplating the world with admiration and delight" while "machinery will be doing all the necessary and unpleasant work."[45]

As technology continued its advance, the idea of "post-scarcity" attained more urgency and the status of a practical utopia. Writing in the USA, then at the forefront of technological development, in the *mid-1960s*, Murray Bookchin could quite rationally discern that after "thousands of years of tortuous development, the countries of the Western world (and potentially all countries) are confronted by the possibility of a materially abundant, almost workless era in which most of the means of life can be provided by machines":

It is easy to foresee a time, by no means remote, when a rationally organized economy could automatically manufacture small 'packaged' factories without human labor; parts could be produced with so little effort that most maintenance tasks would be reduced to the simple act of removing a defective

---

45  Oscar Wilde, *The Soul of Man Under Socialism*, originally published in 1891.

unit from a machine and replacing it by another—a job no
more difficult than pulling out and putting in a tray. Machines
would make and repair most of the machines required to
maintain such a highly industrialised economy. Such a
technology, oriented entirely towards human needs and freed
from all consideration of profit and loss, would eliminate the
pain of want and toil—the penalty, inflicted in the form of
denial, suffering and inhumanity, exacted by a society based
on scarcity and labor. [46]

Since these words were written we have witnessed the
defensive reflexes of a capitalist system determined that
this approaching time is forever seen as remote, both
technologically and imaginatively. Unemployment was
stoked and welfare systems reconfigured to make wage
labour a moral obligation with the threat of destitution
readily at hand should any recalcitrance be encountered. The
focus of the Left was successively shifted from any trace of
an oppositional attitude to an all-encompassing concern with
"social inclusion"—the place of minorities within the system.
Essentially careerism came to be seen as a virtue, not a flaw.
David Graeber in *The Utopia of Rules* suggests that in the 1970s
a profound shift occurred. From investment in "technologies
associated with the possibility of an alternative future" (robot
factories), funds were diverted into the furthering of labour
discipline and social control—information technology that
facilitated financialisation and off-shoring together with

46  Murray Bookchin, *Post-Scarcity Anarchism* (AK Press 2004), 48, 57.
    The essay, "Towards a Liberatory Technology," was written in 1965.

the surveillance and tracking of employees.[47] Meanwhile, organised labour itself was "defanged" in the West and production shifted to low-tech, labour intensive factories in the Global South.

In such a context, the idea that, faced with zero marginal costs, the capitalist system will gleefully walk over the cliff edge, should be met with great scepticism. If economic élites and statesmen have for decades been endeavouring to negate the consequences of technological development—to great success it should be said—they are not suddenly going to throw in the towel. However, zero production costs are still potentially ground-breaking. Firstly, because if they are not implemented it will fatally undermine the notion that capitalism is the most efficient economic system possible. In the real world, the claim that capitalist efficiency rested on the correlation of prices with marginal costs—"one of the most fundamental principles of economics"—always rang hollow. However, behind the textbook models there was the broader contention that capitalist enterprises, under the pressure of competition, naturally seek out the most productive and cost-effective means of manufacturing products and pass on, to some degree, the savings to the consumer. Capitalism was not merely a self-serving system. Its collateral effects—rising generalised wealth and consumer choice—were widespread, self-evident and beneficial. All things considered, and despite its palpable drawbacks, it added to the "general welfare."

However, if for reasons of profit, zero marginal costs are not pursued—or they are pursued but the consumer does

---

47 Graeber, *Utopia of Rules*, 120.

not benefit from them—then a major justification for the existence of an economic order that in other ways generates such obvious social inequities, is lost. Capitalism will be seen as a hindrance to technological development, not its medium. The system's preferred self-image was always that of a dynamic "market"—an impersonal, competitive, lawful order without shareholders, economic power or dominant firms—in which everyone was an equal participant. But in future, the market image is likely to be submerged by the dominant impression of capitalism as simply a system of using whatever economic advantage lies at hand to extract profits for the benefit of élites.[48] The wage system, from being regarded in the past as a regrettable necessity, will come to be seen as a form of domination for which there is no obvious rationale. This loss of legitimacy could prove fatal in the long run, no matter how wealthy and cut off the global elite become.

Secondly, zero marginal costs prefigure the rise of economic entities that are the antithesis of the corporate behemoths that have grown to such seeming invincibility in the global economy. Such giants were called "rational" by Max Weber. This was not primarily because they were the most effective means of making huge profits, but because

---

48  This shift is already apparent. To take one example, according to polls well over half of young people in Australia—a country which emerged from the Great Financial Crisis relatively unscathed—think "capitalism has failed." Peter Boyle, "Poll shows 58% of Millennials in Australia favorable to socialism," *GreenLeft Weekly*, 22 June 2018.

they represented the most efficient method of utilising the available technologies of the day. Centralised, vertically integrated entities, seeking outside capital investment, were required to extract raw materials or fossil fuels, convert them into saleable commodities, and transport them to the customer. Their employees needed to follow strict, non-negotiable instructions. In a sense, the obedience they embodied was a by-product of their economic function. That is why Communist state-owned enterprises and social democratic public corporations largely mimicked their corporate capitalist forebears in their internal organisation. Unquestionably obedience was a welcome side effect—virtually all 20th century political ideologies embraced obedience as they theoretically preached against it—but such centralisation had a grounding in objective reality.

However, the post-scarcity visionaries are now aligned with the grain of economic development in a way that the capitalist corporation is not. It is not possible to say precisely how technology will develop in the future beyond the certainty that it obviously will. 3D printing will become capable of generating more sophisticated products, the capture of renewable energy will become more efficient, the tasks that robots can perform will multiply and encompass cognitive as well as physical operations and miniaturisation and nanotechnology will diminish the need for large-scale physical infrastructures. These breakthroughs will exist regardless of whether they are utilised in the economy. Thus the "rationally organized" economic entity of the near future—rational in the sense that both Max Weber and Murray Bookchin would recognise—will have none of the restraints that encumbered its 20th century forebears. It won't employ large numbers of workers; it won't have to be located in a centralized factory; it will run on renewable energy so it won't be dependent on supplies of gas or coal and it will permit the superabundant production of goods and services at very low cost, while simultaneously requiring minimal capital investment from outside. By implication, the obedience embodied by the first and second industrial revolutions will not grow naturally out of the economic structures of the future.

## The Victory of the Irrational

Of course, just because something is "rational" does not mean it will come to pass. This was Keynes' fallacy. An irrational economic system—in which current structures are preserved not because they are necessary but because they serve the interests of the élite—might seem just as, if not more, probable. The "system of capital accumulation and wage labor is both a technical device for efficient production and a system of power," writes Peter Frace in *Four Futures: Life after Capitalism*. "Having power over others is, for many powerful people, its own reward. Thus, they will endeavor to maintain a system where others serve them, even if such a system is, from a purely productive standpoint, totally superfluous."[49]

However, the attempt to stop the future from happening will face severe challenges, not limited to the conspicuous

---

49  Peter Frace, *Four Futures: Visions of the World After Capitalism* (Verso 2016), 70.

absence of flying cars. The inexorable process—described above—of capital formation, once the source of the system's dynamism and expansion, is now its Achilles' heel. As physical outlets for capital investment—factories and industrial plants—have shrunk, the perpetually growing glut of capital has flooded into financial speculation, as opposed to productive investment, becoming what Marx referred to as "fictitious capital." This financialised system rests perilously at the head of a subdued "real economy" whose instabilities—reduced consumer spending or falling house prices, for example—could set off a wave of financial panic and meltdown. But unless technological progress is completely frozen, production will gradually become more efficient and less in need of capital investment to construct physical productive infrastructures. Therefore capital—which profit always transmutes into—will, even more than now, take a speculative form. With the result that deep economic crises become more likely.

There is another possibility—that humanity definitively enters a post-capitalist era and wage labour is transcended but obedience continues in a non-material form. This is quite possible, even probable. As shown in Chapter 2, early obedience was spiritual. It involved the voluntary assigning of authority to those deemed to have greater knowledge or insight—shamans or elders—while the material base of tribal society remained communal and open to everyone. Tribal "big men" even gave away material possessions in "potlach" ceremonies. In Sumer, the first civilisation, obedience initially had a religious purpose. Only thousands of years later—in the Bronze Age—can obedience be said to grow out of the ownership of a physical resource and become domination by a class. Bronze Age princes like Agamemnon and Achilles could live in ornate palaces and fight wars for treasure because of numberless peasants who tilled their land and herded their flocks. Murray Bookchin saw, earlier than anyone in the modern age, the potential of "post-scarcity" and a "rationally organized economy." But his political project evolved into an attempt to dispense with of all forms of hierarchy. Defeating class society, ridding the world of exploitation and the monopolisation of property by an élite, was not enough. Hierarchies, "subtle and elusive phenomena" around age, gender, ethnicity or bureaucratic control, had to be confronted.[50] If they weren't, they would merely be carried unconsciously into a classless, but far from utopian, future.

In other words, while material, concrete systems of power can be overcome, the subjective, psychological basis of obedience might linger. This process can be observed historically. The "free" labourer, no longer tied to the manor or the village, and theoretically the controller of his own destiny, became the foot-soldier of the joint stock companies and corporations of the 19th century. But what made these organisations function efficiently was undoubtedly older, feudal forms of deference—obedience to one's "betters" and "masters." Supposedly advanced capitalist countries, such as Britain and Germany, were still immensely status-ridden as well as class-ridden well into the 20th century. In the 1960s historian Peter Laslett argued that the status-obsessed world of 17th century England retained a "ghostly persistence"

---

50 Bookchin, *Ecology of Freedom*, 28.

centuries later, and was "in some sense still present with us."[51] If human beings aren't blank slates, merely the totality of historically determined social relations, then what is inscribed on their consciousness cannot simply be rubbed out in the twinkling of an eye.

Following Bookchin, therefore, we need to embrace the potential of material abundance—"sufficiency in the means of life without the need for grinding, day-to-day toil"—whilst acknowledging its limitations.[52] For post-scarcity does represent an existential threat to obedience. If behaviour is no longer governed by the requirement to placate élites in order to survive or prosper, then the gradations of society are no longer predictable. Or from another angle, if the material underpinnings of the mass of people are assured, then threats of destitution or promises of plenty will not have the same efficacy that they did in the past. In this sense, a post-scarcity economy—or finally solving what used to be termed "the social question"—will have implications far beyond workplace relations, consumer behaviour or mental health. It is perverse to believe that domestic arrangements, education or the media—to name a few arenas—will not be transformed too. But the prime area for metamorphosis will be the realm that, since the 19th century, we have been content to call "democracy."

---

51  Laslett, *The World We Have Lost*, 25.

52  Bookchin, *Post-Scarcity Anarchism*, iv.

# Chapter Four

# The Disobedient Society

Hannah Arendt is a philosopher who is hard to pin down. She is most famous for the aphorism "the banality of evil," used to describe Adolf Eichmann, the Nazi executed in 1962 for his role in organising the Holocaust. As we saw in Chapter 1, Stanley Milgram was inspired by this image of a person reduced to a cog in the machine, unquestioningly obeying the genocidal orders of superiors. His investigation into the psychological roots of "obedience to authority" was even dubbed the "Eichmann experiment" by a colleague. However, this premise was a simplification, even a distortion of what

Arendt was saying. She never denied that Eichmann was an idealistic Nazi. The banality of evil was really about how evil purposes insert themselves in the world, and become seen as logical, just and the way of the majority. Eichmann personified this acceptance, this "going-along-with," as Arendt put it. Besides being a fervent Nazi, Eichmann was a thoughtless careerist, possessed of an "extraordinary diligence in looking out for his personal advancement."[1] And the blindness of careerism is not peculiar to Nazi Germany. It is now seen as natural and good, a thoroughly innocent way of engaging with the world.

But Arendt's opaqueness is not limited to how she viewed Eichmann. She was also a theorist of the revolutionary tradition and viewed the history of the European revolutions in ways that defied simple definition. The gist of her 1963 book, *On Revolution*, was thoroughly conservative. Compassion for the abject poverty of "the people" doomed the French Revolution, leading directly to the Guillotine and the Terror. Subsequent revolutions, such as the Russian, followed the same fateful trajectory for the same reason. The American Revolution of the 1770s and 1780s, by contrast, was successful precisely because it didn't try to improve the condition of the people. It was consciously confined to changing the form of government and thus didn't devour itself. Though as Arendt partially admitted, American revolutionaries could only do this because the freedom of their new Republic was built on black slavery and misery.

---

1    Hannah Arendt, *Eichmann in Jerusalem* (Penguin Books 2006), 287.

146

But after making this argument which could only appeal to the conservative mind-set, *On Revolution* takes an unexpected turn.[2] Arendt turns her attention to the American revolutionary Thomas Jefferson's unrealised plan for a system of "ward republics" in which every person could be a "participator in government." Such "elementary republics" would, together with county, state and federal republics, form a "gradation of authorities" and "collect the voice of the people" in a far more authentic way than the mechanics of representative government could ever hope to.[3] "Every man [sic] in the State," said Jefferson, could become "an acting member of the Common government, transacting in person a great portion of its rights and duties."[4]

Arendt does not cite Jefferson's theorizing as evidence of the superiority of American democracy over European totalitarianism. Quite the opposite. She asserts that all modern European revolutions—the French, the 1871 Paris Commune, the Russian Revolutions of 1905 and 1917, the

---

2   Former British Conservative Prime Minister Margaret Thatcher, never one to suffer from a surfeit of compassion, viewed the French Revolution as a project of "vain intellectuals" leading inexorably to mass murder. The American Declaration of Independence, by contrast, was "one of the most brilliant pieces of English literature" which asserted that the purpose of government was to serve the liberties of mankind. Stephen Thompson, "Bastille Day and Margaret Thatcher," *The British-American Conservative*, 14 July, 2014.

3   Hannah Arendt, *On Revolution* (Faber & Faber, 2016), 258.

4   Quoted in ibid.

German Revolution of 1918-19, the Spanish Revolution of 1936-7 and the Hungarian Revolution of 1956—created "a new form of government that resembled in an amazing fashion Jefferson's ward system". This was the communal council system of popular democracy—the sections of revolutionary Paris, the *soviets* of Russia and the workers' and soldiers' *räte* of Germany. (Both *soviets* and *Räte* mean councils in English).

The revolutionary councils unfailingly appeared at the same time and in the same places as the revolutionary party system and its efforts to seize state power (Robespierre and the Jacobins, Lenin and the Bolsheviks). In the German Revolution of 1918-19, even the Conservative party was compelled to accept the existence of the Räte in its election campaigns. But while the revolutionary parties have become synonymous with the concept of revolution, the councils "an entirely new form of government … which was constituted and organized during the course of the revolution itself… have been "utterly neglected by statesmen, historians, political theorists and, most importantly, by the revolutionary tradition itself."[5] Thus, Arendt was saying, we have completely misunderstood what a revolution is.

## The Real Soviets

Far from sounding a conservative warning about the inherent dangers of revolution, Arendt was marking out a position *to the Left of the revolutionary Left*. Lenin ignited the October Revolution in Russia with his famous cry, "All

---

5    Ibid, p 252-3

power to the soviets!", yet within three years the Bolsheviks had so thoroughly enfeebled them as independent entities, that they ceased to have any genuine existence. The fact that the country emerging from the Russian Revolution was called "The *Soviet* Union" was both testimony to the hidden nature of the revolution, and a gross deception out of which eventually emerged a totalitarian, party-controlled state and the polar opposite of the popular democracy.

However, all political tendencies—liberal, conservative and Marxist—have colluded in this deception. When they are not simply overlooked, the councils and soviets are seen either as fleeting outpourings of utopian desire or temporary instruments to drive the revolution forward to be dispensed with once they have served their historic purpose. But the actual revolutionary councils conceived of themselves in quite a different way. They thought they should be a permanent part of the landscape, "a new form of government", in Arendt's words. This can be observed in the "extraordinary historical coincidence" that supplies the title of Murray Bookchin's four volume history of the revolutionary era—*The Third Revolution*. Both the sans-culottes in Paris in 1793 and the "red sailors" of Kronstadt in 1921 raised the cry for a "Third Revolution"; the restoration of popular democracy—the former to replace the National Convention and the latter to overthrow the authoritarian rule of the Bolsheviks.[6] They were anything but ephemeral.

---

6    Murray Bookchin, *The Third Revolution: Popular Movements in the Revolutionary Era*, Volume 1 (Cassell, 1996), 1. The first revolution involved the overthrow of the monarchy—Louis XVI in France and Tsar Nicholas II in Russia.

What distinguished the councils was not just their infinite variety—there were factory committees for workers, soldiers' councils, peasant assemblies, councils for young people, artists, even civil servants—but that they were consciously designed for participation, rather than obedience to an agreed line and course of action defined by the political parties. Everyone was entitled to speak and be heard. Their officials were subject to rotation and recall, and they elected delegates to higher councils and who elected deputies to still higher bodies. Their revolutionary character stemmed precisely from this openness and accountability. Arendt located this "revolutionary spirit" in the internal affairs of the Parisian sections of the French Revolution:

> In the by-laws of one of the Parisian sections we hear, for instance, how the people organized themselves into a society— with president and vice-president, four secretaries, eight censors, a treasurer and an archivist; with regular meetings, three in every ten days; with rotation in office, once a month for the president; how they defined its main task: "The society will deal with everything that concerns freedom, equality, indivisibility of the republic; [its members] will enlighten themselves on the respect due to the laws and decrees which are promulgated"; how they intended to keep order in their discussion: if a speaker digresses or gets tiresome, the audience will stand up.[7]

---

7    Ibid., 245.

## The Illusion of Representation

Arendt's argument—awkwardly—was not merely against the one-party communist dictatorships that arose from revolution and, at the time of her writing (the early 1960s), exhibited a solid and depressing durability. She was also hostile to "modern party government" itself—the representative, ostensibly democratic governments that ruled America and West European nation-states. These governments were, in reality, oligarchies—communication between representative and voter, where it genuinely existed, was "never between equals but between those who aspire to govern and those who consent to be governed."[8] And consent—the ability to ratify or not ratify a choice you are presented with—is, as Arendt observed, an entirely different beast to participation.

The neoliberal era—which coincidentally began almost immediately after Arendt's death in 1975 –has hypostatized consent into the *sine qua non* of legitimate power, both economically and politically. Economically, the bestowing of consent marks the all-important dividing line between exchange and theft and between free wage labour and forced labour or modern-day slavery. This holds despite the fact that propertylessness or welfare conditionality invariably leaves those who give consent with no choice but to grant it to someone. And once consent has been obtained, the relationship between employer and employee is one of

---

8   Ibid., 281.

control, of following orders, of obedience.[9] However, as long as the labour contract is voluntary—or rather perceived as voluntary on all sides—it is, to neoliberals, a manifestation of freedom and should not be interfered with.

Politically, the idea of consent powered the spread of free and multi-party elections across the world from the fall of the Berlin Wall in 1989 until the early part of the 21st century. But, as with the economy, the imperative was to gain the consent of the governed to a non-negotiable set of policies, not to ensure the fulfilment of democratic mandates. Governments, once they had entered office with the consent of the people, were ensconced in a "golden straitjacket" which narrowed "the political and economic choices of those in power to relatively tight parameters"—epitomised by low corporate taxes, liberalised financial markets and balanced budgets.[10] Should any country fail to respect the boundaries of this "market-friendly democracy" they need to be brought into line with the devastating judgement of credit-rating agencies and/or austerity regimes overseen by pan-governmental agencies

---

9    An additional problem for the "capitalism rests on consent" position is that those on the margins of the global economy often consent to blatantly coercive practices such as trafficking or debt bondage because, in circumstances of extreme propertylessness, they represent the "least worst option." See Neil Howard, "Capitalism, coercion and modern-day abolition," *Basic Income*, May 2015.

10    The term is from New York Times columnist Thomas Friedman's book, *The Lexus and the Olive Tree* (Anchor Books, 1999). The straitjacket still exists but it's not golden anymore.

like the IMF.[11] However, the consent of the voters—ideally their repeated consent—for policies often diametrically opposed to their wishes was craved. The public had to want what it didn't want. One-party dictatorship—the disavowal of any need for consent—was to be avoided at all costs.

The treatment of post-2010 Greece by the troika of the EU, European Central Bank (ECB) and International Monetary Fund illustrates this mentality perfectly. The left-wing Syriza party won the January 2015 elections on a mandate of ending the crushing austerity and privatisation programme imposed as a condition of the EU-bail out (the largest loan in human history, with repayments transferred to insolvent French and German banks). Almost immediately the ECB ended emergency support to Greek banks, prompting a bank run and paving the way for Syriza's submission. Following the troika's refusal in the summer of 2015 to accept a referendum rejection of the bail-out terms, Syriza utterly folded and accepted a package of larger spending cuts and tax increases than it had put before the Greek people in the referendum.

Thus, an ostensibly leftist political party was boxed into a position where it agreed to continue with extreme austerity (termed "fiscal waterboarding" by Yanis Varoufakis), and the sale of thousands of state assets to the private sector—policies utterly at odds with its professed beliefs and democratic

---

11　The latest manifestation of this policy is the IMF's $57 billion bail-out of Argentina, agreed in late September 2018. Conditions include eradicating the government budget deficit by 2019 and draconian restrictions on when the Argentinian central bank can intervene in the economy.

mandate. In January 2018, Syriza, under pressure from the European Commission, even introduced the most punitive restrictions on the right to strike in Europe.[12] As the third bail-out programme came to an end in August 2018, the government was warned by its central bank governor that "markets are waiting" to see if its resolve to see through further "reforms"—including yet another round of pension cuts and the privatisation of electricity provision—would prove strong enough.[13] However, integral to the whole process, Syriza, or its predecessors, never suspended Parliamentary government. Greek "democracy" and periodic free and multi-party elections were not infringed—the next Greek Parliamentary elections went ahead, even earlier than planned, in July 2019. They were won by the conservative New Democracy party, which promised even greater privatisation of public services. Greeks always had a choice—they consented to their own pain.

## The Red Thread

Arendt was struck by the "sameness of the phenomenon" in all revolutions.[14] Institutions of self-management habitually arose in spite of the absence of tradition, continuity or conscious imitation. It is almost as if the sudden break

12  Under the new law, strikes require affirmation from more than half of all workers in a workplace, regardless of turnout. This is higher than the 40% threshold for certain public services introduced by the Conservatives in Britain in 2016.

13  "Athens told to stick to reforms or risk losing investment," *Financial Times*, 31 July 2018.

14  Arendt, *On Revolution*, 266.

down of established custom and authority stirred ancestral memories that materialized in remarkably similar ways. But this repetition was not unique to the two hundred year era of European revolutions. As a thinker steeped in the ethos of the ancient Greek polis, Arendt would have been quite aware of the correspondences between the revolutionary councils and Athenian direct democracy. Both were founded on the primacy of discussion and persuasion as opposed to force and violence. She called the polis the "sphere of freedom," while designating the councils "spaces of freedom."[15]

The Athenian polis explicitly invoked tribal memories. The ecclesia—the popular assembly—was a revived tribal institution and the population of Athens was divided into ten territorial "tribes" which supplied members, chosen by sortition, for the executive council, the boule. The Athens' "revolution" entailed returning, albeit in altered fashion, to the tribal past. This was a past in which, thousands of years previously, the assembly had been sovereign. The Mesopotamian cities of Sumer, the first civilisation in history, were originally controlled by popular assemblies. An anthropologist who examined their character claimed they resembled, in their "assumption that every citizen is concerned with the common weal," the cities of Greece, the Hanseatic League and Renaissance Italy.[16]

---

15  Hannah Arendt, *The Human Condition* (University of Chicago Press, 1958), 30; Arendt, *On Revolution*, 268.

16  Henri Frankfort, *The Birth of Civilization in the Near East* (Doubleday Anchor Books, 1956), 77.

Go the other way in time—that is, post-1989—and similar ruptures with established power reveal themselves. In Argentina in 2001, in what was dubbed "the first rebellion against neoliberalism in the 21st century," an economic crisis prompted the spontaneous creation of hundreds of popular assemblies across the country—120 in the capital Buenos Aires alone. It was estimated that one-third of residents in the capital participated in an assembly or an activity organised by one. Members met daily or weekly to discuss the crisis, plan mobilizations against multi-national companies or the government and alleviate the negative effects the crisis was having on the population. Assemblies began to organise free kitchens, nurseries and community bakeries and participate in the factory take-over movement. Some permanently occupied their own spaces within buildings.

The Argentinian assemblies also made attempts at achieving a "gradation of authorities" and sent delegates to a city-wide assembly in Buenos Aires known as the *Asamblea Interbarrial*. This assembly, attracting thousands of attendees, met several times and passed resolutions on matters of national importance. The assembly movement, however, underwent a fatal decline following government concessions to its supporters—addressing problems that had led them to form assemblies in the first place—and the attempt by political parties to coopt it.

The most far-reaching alternative to consensual representation in the 21st century, though, is still ongoing. This is the system of "democratic confederalism" established in the northern Syrian region of Rojava and surrounding areas.[17] Beginning in 2012 just after the devastating civil war began, a council system took root with the aim of disseminating popular wishes up through a series of levels, from the residential street, then neighbourhoods and cities, to an entire region. This is in flat contradiction to the consensual representative system we have learnt to call democracy, where the power of the public is limited to periodically ratifying the decisions of representatives at the level of the nation-state or the municipality.

The base level of the Rojavan system, known as the "commune," is the street or, in the countryside, a whole village. A commune consists of 30-200 households in cities. Every one or two months, everyone living in the commune is invited to an open assembly meeting and to talk about whatever concerns them. The commune elects a coordinating board, one man and one woman, who meet weekly. Every resident can take part in these meeting—to listen or make a criticism or suggestion.

The two-person commune coordinating board then attends a neighbourhood council, comprising 7-30 communes. For example, Hesekê, a city in north-eastern Syria with a population of 188,000, has 16 neighbourhood councils. Delegates from the communes to the councils are subject to an obligatory mandate—they can't just do what they want but have to try to reflect the view of their commune. If they fail to do this, they can be recalled. Every neighbourhood and village also has a "people's house" (*mala*

---

17  The summary that follows is mainly gleaned from *Revolution in Rojava* by Michael Knapp, Anja Flach and Ercan Ayboga (Pluto Press, 2016).

*gel)* which is open and guarded 24 hours a day and in which all political issues can be discussed.

The neighbourhood councils elect their own coordinating a board in each case—one man and one woman, subject to mandates—who attend a district council, which encompasses a whole city and the villages in its environs. The district council, consisting of 100-200 people, elects its own coordinating body known as the TEV-DEM ("Movement for a Democratic Society"). The district councils control Rojava's municipal administrations and have responsibility for services such as refuse collection and water supply. The coordinating bodies of the district councils then attend the highest level—the People's Council of West Kurdistan (MGRK). The MGRK elects a council for the whole of Rojava.

However, the Rojavan system of "democratic autonomy" does not end there. There are also eight "commissions" at each of the four council levels. The commissions are dedicated to areas such as women, defence, the economy, politics and justice. Members of the women's communes visit local women in their homes and encourage them to get involved in political activities as well as forming women's cooperatives. The defence commissions are the first line of defence if a neighbourhood is attacked. The economics commissions are concerned with the supply of food, oil and gas, the creation of cooperatives and the management of public enterprises. There are justice commissions which deal with land ownership disputes, road traffic accidents and other more serious misdemeanours.

Although sophisticated, the Rojavan council system is not the "finished article." In the circumstances of a brutal civil war, possibly the most destructive conflict since World War Two, everything is fluid. The council system first flourished in Aleppo, a city outside of Rojava which before the war had a population of two million. However, due to bombardment by the forces of the Assad regime and the Free Syrian Army beginning in 2013, the councils have mostly been suppressed. Up to 90% of the 200,000 population of Afrîn, a Rojavan canton, participated in the council system, until that is the Turkish invasion and occupation of early 2018.

The council system also operates alongside a nascent state structure, the existing Ba'athist state infrastructure having been dismantled after the 2011 uprising. In 2014, the three Rojavan cantons—Afrîn, Jazirah and Kobane—each formed transitional administrations with Parliaments and executive councils. The executive councils have ministries, such as for social affairs or the environment, and the ministers are from political parties. The Democratic-Autonomous Administrations, as they are known, have helped overcome ethnic and religious prejudice between Kurds, Christians and Sunni Arabs. They have formally stated their support for the communes, but how they practically co-exist with the MGRK council system remains to be definitively determined.

However, the Rojavan councils—like the soviets of the Russia Revolution and the Parisian sections of 1790-5—aspire to permanence, to become, in Arendt's description, "a new form of government." The number of new communes is continually growing in Rojava. And in areas of Syria liberated by the Syrian Democratic Forces (a multi-ethnic military alliance led by the Kurdish People's Protection Units which at the time of writing controls over a quarter of Syrian territory) the offer to develop the council system is always made. The creation of a democratic *society*—"self-administrative regions based on councils, academies, communes and cooperatives"— rather than separation and state-building, is intended to be the model for the whole of Syria.[18] And beyond.

## Freedom as Power

"The capacity of a revolution to produce far-reaching ideological and moral changes in a people," wrote Murray Bookchin in *The Third Revolution*, "stems primarily from the opportunity it affords ordinary, indeed oppressed, people to … enter directly, rapidly, and exhilaratingly into control over most aspects of their social and personal lives." This sense of "freedom-as-power," as the English writer Dan Hind calls it, is intoxicating. But the feeling of exhilaration and power does not flow from an individual release from ethical constraints, a lifting of behavioural sanctions or the sudden opportunity to slake previously unfulfilled desires. Society and authority does not cease to exist. In Rojava there is a popularly-controlled "police force" known as the Asayiş, people's courts at the district level with judges elected by the commune and the maintenance of municipal services such as refuse collection. However, its ethical scope broadens immensely—the perspective of each

---

18  From the formal statement of federation by the three Rojavan cantons creating the "Democratic Federation of Rojava—Northern Syria," March 2016 (available in English at rojavanorthernsyria.noblogs.org).

person is recognised as valid and worth hearing. Politics, says Hind, ceases to be something to be watched from a distance and becomes something one does.[19]

The pool of collective intelligence in society, which usually exists unseen and unheard, is abruptly revealed to be a vast resource which can guide and improve it. Such a revelation is in direct contradiction to the basic assumption of our consensual societies where intelligence is thought to reside exclusively in the upper echelons of society—among business leaders, entrepreneurs, the wealthy, celebrities, successful actors, politicians and media commentators. It is their voices that rise above all others. The rest of society—the bottom 30% in particular—are thought to lack the requisite talent, grit and leadership qualities, and so are essentially mute. Their role is to copy the "habits of highly effective people," as the best-selling book title advocates.[20] Unemployment and, frequently disability, are repackaged as stemming from psychological flaws, to be overcome by a concerted attempt to develop new habits. However, the underlying understanding is that, for most, the imitation of the successful will only be of limited use. "The harder you shake the pack, the easier it will be for some cornflakes to get to the top," said the British Conservative and current Prime Minister, Boris Johnson, in 2013. This is a toxic mix—we are responsible for our own failings yet powerless

---

19  Dan Hind, *The Magic Kingdom: Property, Monarchy, and the Maximum Republic* (Zero Books, 2016), 107.

20  Stephen Covey, *The 7 Habits of Highly Effective People*, which aimed to teach "self-mastery," was first published by the Free Press in 1989.

to make any meaningful changes in the circumstances of our lives, which are "rigidly determined," in the words of Karl Polanyi, by the laws of the market. Anxiety and depression, which both feed on a sense of powerlessness and helplessness, have become the trademark mental states of this society.

In an age of free elections and the internet, unruly mass desires—ones that don't merely mimic entrepreneurial homilies—cannot be completely controlled. But they can be channelled into safe directions for the powerful. Donald Trump personifies this channelling. A billionaire, he rides on whipping up ethnic fear and resentment, yet delivers, simultaneously, huge tax cuts for corporations and the wealthy. The implication is that, as it did in the 1930s, society can go in increasingly malevolent, dark directions whilst preserving structures and economic regimes which feed the wealth of the already powerful. The archetype here is Adolf Hitler, who suppressed anti-capitalist elements in the Nazi movement in order to cement his appeal to big business and, once in power, enacted the world's first privatisation programme, destroyed organised labour and abolished collective bargaining.[21] Far from being incompatible with free enterprise, Nazism—from the moment it entered power

---

21  See Germà Bel, "Against the Mainstream: Nazi privatization in 1930s Germany," *Economic History Review*, 63: 1 (2010), 34-55. Bel argues that, although modern economic literature fails to notice it, the Nazis divested themselves of public ownership in many firms, in several sectors. The aim was to bolster support among industrialists and the business sector despite this policy being contrary to National Socialism's official economic programme.

until its apogee in orgies of destruction and genocide—rested on private ownership, profit and exploitation.

In the 1970s, Stanley Milgram thought he had demonstrated how humanity had evolved to function within hierarchical structures. Such structures were, to Milgram, the mainstays of social life itself. People learn obedience, he said, through operating within seemingly innocuous institutions such as schools, business or the church. They learn to function, benignly at first, as a "subordinate element in an authority system."[22] However, the reason why Milgram embarked on his obedience experiments in the first place was the disturbing evidence that these hierarchical structures could come to be controlled by sinister forces which channelled irrational emotions and hatreds. Thus the "natural" obedience they elicited among ordinary people could be exploited by those who commanded the structure to engineer atrocities and genocide. While perpetual vigilance might ensure this didn't happen, obedience itself was written in our genes. A social structure that wasn't hierarchically-organised, that didn't segregate its members into subordinate and superordinate roles, and that therefore didn't rely on obedience was, to Milgram, an impossibility.

Thus Rojava and the democratic councils of the classical European revolutions *should not happen*. They are against "human nature." The inescapable fact that they do happen, and keep recurring, must be explained by the extreme circumstances surrounding their appearance—the deprivations and shock of war, economic trauma, the vacuum created by the sudden disappearance of traditional, civil

---

22 Milgram, *Obedience to Authority*, 138.

authority and power. They are historical freaks which do not arise under the normal course of events. According to this dominant view—with adherents on the political right, centre and left—once these impractical, utopian exercises in mass democracy confront the harsh realities of the reproduction of social life, they melt away like ice left out in the sun.

However, if the council system does not run counter to "human nature"—if it is as much a product of human nature as the state and hierarchical social structures ("the council system seems to correspond to and to spring from the very experience of political action" said Hannah Arendt)—then different questions are begged.[23] If the councils didn't die because of a profound unfitness to deal with the inevitable but commonplace needs of millions of people—if they were just as viable as the structures that replaced them and, in fact, aspired to permanence—then an alternative explanation is required. The answer demanded is not to "why did the councils appear?" but to "why did they disappear?"

## The Social Question

Arendt's answer satisfied no-one. She was convinced that the council system was an unerring feature of all revolutions—"the authentic outgrowth of every revolution since the eighteenth century."[24] But her contention was that the councils were simultaneously doomed by the overriding purpose of

---

23  From "Thoughts on Politics and Revolution," in *Hannah Arendt: The Last Interview* (Melville House Publishing, 2013), 103.

24  Arendt, *Crises of the Republic,* 124.

revolution itself—that of resolving the "social question." The social question arose from the existence of vast numbers of poor and hungry human beings—how to liberate them and create a social system that didn't have poverty and want as its defining characteristics was the issue that both fomented revolution and became its task to solve.

Karl Marx personified this split. He was, according to Arendt, "the greatest theorist the revolutions ever had" and was obsessed with the social question, believing a failure to deal with it doomed the French Revolution. All future revolutions had to avoid this fate and, politically seize control of the state, paving the way for a social system beyond capitalism. But Marx also thought that the councils of the Paris Commune of 1871 might be "the political form, finally discovered, for the economic liberation of labour"—that is, a timeless form of freedom that arose during a phase of revolution but before society's economic and social structures had been totally revolutionised. Lenin, too, stated that the essence of the Russian Revolution was "electrification plus soviets"—note the use of soviets, in plural, the institutions of direct democracy, not a state controlled by a Communist party that implements socialism.

An obvious objection to Arendt's logic is how could it have been otherwise? How could the revolutions of the 19th and 20th centuries not have been obsessed with settling the social question, with dealing with the immense human misery in their midst; an obsession, it should be stressed, that extended to the councils themselves who were not mere debating clubs but sought radical changes in society. Arendt was not prone to argue on this point. Although she affirms that "every attempt to solve the social question with political means leads to terror," she concedes that "to avoid this fatal mistake is almost impossible when a revolution breaks out under conditions of mass poverty."[25] However, on the fundamental argument, she remained unmoved. The councils, the political expressions of freedom, were devastated by the use of political means to resolve the social question. This was so because, to Arendt, two incompatible concepts were battling it out to become the "spirit of revolution"—freedom and necessity.

It is as well to understand the conflict Arendt discerned between freedom and necessity because on that question hinges, not just the explanation for why revolutions of the past devoured themselves, but the fate of future (and current) revolutions as well. To Arendt, the councils were "spaces of freedom" because they epitomised exchanging opinions, listening to others and forming agreement—they were venues of persuasion, not of compulsion. Necessity, on the other hand, responded only to force—it required the satisfaction of basic biological needs such as hunger and shelter and thus brooked no debate. It was profoundly apolitical. Poverty is more than deprivation, said Arendt; it places men and women in a state of such acute misery that they are dehumanised and "under the absolute dictates of their bodies."[26]

The islands of freedom in history were dependent on submerging necessity—basically by placing the task of reproducing life on the shoulders of others. The ancient Greek polis could exist as a "sphere of freedom" explicitly because

---

25  Arendt, *On Revolution*, 110.

26  Ibid., 54.

ownership of slaves and patriarchal control of households freed male Athenian citizens from the "sphere of necessity." "The freedom of the political realm," said Arendt, "begins after all elementary necessities of sheer living have been mastered by rule, so that domination and subjection, command and obedience, ruling and being ruled, are conditions for establishing the political realm precisely because they are not its content."[27] Even a legally free man could be forced by poverty to "act like a slave."[28] Thus, always in history, a minority could achieve freedom only by "forcing others to bear the burden of life for them."[29] This was the core of all "ruler-ship" and its manifestations such as chattel slavery.

To Arendt, the revolutions of the 19th and 20th centuries were still swimming in the stream of this history even as they endeavoured to transcend it. This ambition was their essential problem. Had they been content to limit themselves to establishing political forms to fight autocracy or foreign domination—as the American Revolution had—they would not have descended into terror and totalitarianism. But they destroyed themselves in trying overcome necessity, in the attempt "to liberate the life process of society from the fetters of scarcity so that it could swell into a stream of abundance."[30] Abundance, rather than freedom, says Arendt, "now became the aim of revolution."

---

27 From "What is Authority?" in *The Portable Hannah Arendt* (Penguin, 2003), 483-484.

28 Arendt, *The Human Condition*, 64.

29 Arendt, *On Revolution*, 110.

30 Ibid., 58.

This aim was seen by revolutionists such as Marx as the precondition for freedom, not its nemesis. Burdened by material want, the mass of people had to renounce their new-found visibility and power after the initial euphoric phase of revolutions—they had to go back to work and return the management of society to professional politicians and owners of property. So technological development, liberation from scarcity, was essential—without it all equalisation would do would generalise want. But the irony was the mass of people had to temporarily leave the stage of history while this technological development occurred.

The lesson of the classical European revolutions was that once they left, they never came back. Society became dominated either by the private owners of land and factories or Communist party apparatchiks. In Marxist terms, socialism—a state-managed economy—never gave way to communism, a stateless, self-managed, technically advanced system, and never remotely looked like doing so. The vast majority became mute once again—to be spoken on behalf of, represented or consoled with being a force of history, the ultimate beneficiaries of denial and sacrifice. Arendt regarded this outcome as preordained by the nature of revolution—"no revolution has ever solved the 'social question' and liberated men [sic] from the predicament of want," she said.[31] What could do, she suggested, was a neutral, apolitical force—"the rise of technology" and economic growth itself.

The implication of Arendt's thinking is that once technological progress has reached a certain peak, freedom can

---

31  Ibid., 108.

be universalised. Throughout history, the sphere of freedom has been the privilege of small minorities, forged by banishing the many to the sphere of necessity where they labour to produce the "elementary necessities of sheer living" so that freedom can exist for the few. But this seemingly indissoluble tie between freedom on the one hand and command and obedience on the other could be exploded by technology, "the slavery of the machine" in Oscar Wilde's phrase. Then, the sphere of freedom could be opened to everyone. However, this process cannot be forced by political means, Arendt argued. It had to arise through neutral economic development.

She did consider such a possibility—that, through leaps in productivity, the freedom of the Athenian polis could be realised "without slaves to sustain itself but would become a reality for all."[32] Naturally perhaps, given her enigmatic philosophical reputation, she found it sorely lacking. In fact, the possibility had become reality in the America of the late 1950s. The "liberation of the productive forces" of society had, according to Arendt, already happened. But she looked around at the *animal laborans* (her derogatory term for humans distinguished from animals merely by their propensity to labour) and found that, freed from necessity, they devoted all their spare time to consumption. This was not utopia but a "fool's paradise." Consumption, no longer restricted to the necessities of life, "does not change the character of this society," she asserted, "but harbors the grave danger that eventually no object will be safe from consumption and annihilation through consumption."[33]

---

32  Arendt, *The Human Condition*, 133.

33  Ibid.

Arendt was firmly trapped within the liberal mentality (ironically because she wasn't a liberal) which assumes that capitalist accumulation is propelled by the desires of consumers rather than, as seen in chapter 3, having an independent life of its own. Notwithstanding Arendt's disappointment in humanity—replicated a thousand times since—gratuitous consumption is an outcome, not a cause. Economic growth and consumption will go on indefinitely— until "eventually no object will be safe from ... annihilation through consumption"—because the economic system, in a grim circular logic, demands that profits are reinvested to make more profits which are then invested again. Marxists have understood this process very well. But Arendt understood things they generally don't. That a political realm exists, that the need for politics doesn't evaporate when the material conditions for freedom have been met and that politics—defined as discussion, debate and the exchange of opinions—has a purpose of its own beyond the immediate urgency to use political means to repress resistance to communism, socialism or however a post-capitalist society is defined.[34]

Reading Arendt, the existence of two distinct revolutionary traditions becomes clear. The dominant one is primarily Marxist and driven by the need to establish the material preconditions of freedom. It sees power as a form of organised force aimed at repressing elements intent on destroying the revolution and seeks to deploy the state to bring about economic development. The second, less conspicuous, cherishes freedom in the here and now, regards

34  See Rossi, *A Politics for the 99%*, 15-31.

power as separate from violence and sees politics—people speaking and acting together—as an essential feature of a free society.[35] The two traditions have often intermingled, albeit unconsciously.[36] But they are discrete, even contradictory.

In a future revolution, the second tradition will have to come to the fore. What makes this easier is that society lies on the verge of solving "the social question," the inescapability of which, Arendt believed, sent the revolutions of the past to their doom.

## A Post-Work Society and Unconditional Income

It is an arguable question of counter-factual history whether the revolutionary councils, notwithstanding their desire to

---

35  Power, said, Arendt, involves people getting together and "acting in concert." It requires a sense of the legitimacy of action. For her distinction between power and violence—which she regarded as opposites—see Chapter 2.

36  Marx and Lenin did, unconsciously, veer between the two traditions. Other political currents—such as council communism— did so explicitly. For example, Sylvia Pankhurst, the English suffragette, universal suffrage campaigner and socialist saw the council element as an essential part of communism. In the wake of the Russian Revolution, she advocated the creation of "social soviets" in Britain, based on areas in which people lived rather than where they worked. Delegates, not representatives, would be "constantly reporting back and getting instructions from their constituents." See Shirley Harrison, *Sylvia Pankhurst: The Rebellious Suffragette* (Golden Guides Press, 2012), 286.

become a new form of government, could have survived and directed the course of public affairs had they not been consciously suppressed. To suggest that the cards were stacked against them from the beginning is not to subscribe to the jaded political realism denigrated by Arendt—the conviction that a people simply cannot govern itself and "there is not, and never has been, any alternative to the present system."[37] The councils were not impossible social forms brought into tragic and ephemeral existence by extraordinary circumstances. But there was a palpable discrepancy between their ambition— that everyone who wishes to should be able to participate in the forming of public policy and the future course of society—and the economic realities that surrounded them. They took place in societies of scarcity, in an era dominated, in Arendtian language, by the "sphere of necessity." Simply put: genuine participation takes time and will inevitably degenerate into the rule of professional politicians if the mass of people have to spend most of their waking hours working or caring for others. This was undeniably a limitation of the classical Europeans revolutions—if you have to get up to go to work at 5 in the morning, you are unlikely to be able to take part in a neighbourhood meeting that goes on late into the night.[38] Revolutionary fervour can fuel participatory

---

37  Arendt, *On Revolution*, 274-275.

38  For example, attendance at the meetings of the sections during
   the French Revolution rarely exceeded 10% of the citizenry
   and the section committees, which met in the afternoon, were
   dominated by people with independent incomes. According to
   Bookchin, labourers living in poor and overcrowded conditions

institutions beyond the normal limits of endurance—much like a person can call on unexpected reserves of stamina and strength in emergencies. But it cannot last forever.

This is not an arcane historical matter. David Graeber has observed at first hand the revolution in Rojava. This is a genuine revolution which has, as can be seen by the description above, put in place a system of open meetings intended to capture popular feelings and opinions and transmit them upwards through a series of levels, ending in the government of an entire region. Arguably "democratic confederalism," as it is known, is the most extensive attempt in history to attempt this feat—the base level of the Rojavan system is the residential street. But not being a simple consensual, representative system, the "activists" in the Rojavan councils must constantly consult to make sure they are reflecting the views of those below them in the system. This is inevitably extremely time-consuming:

> Local assemblies confederate to neighbourhood assemblies, by sending two delegates each, male and female (each attached working group such as health, education, security, also sends its own two delegates and so does the all-woman group associated with each), and then those neighbourhood groups each

> "could hardly have participated actively in running revolutionary institutions or attending assembly meetings regularly, especially when so many of those meetings overlapped with their working hours. … their ability to mold events and decide policies was patently limited." Bookchin, *The Third Revolution*, 323.

likewise send two delegates to municipal assemblies. These are delegates, it was emphasised, not representatives. They must consult about everything, they cannot make decisions on their own. But this means that anyone in a municipal assembly has to engage in three different groups, on three different levels, and if they are in a municipal working group at least six! Since meetings are long, it's hard to imagine how anyone not free to dedicate a large percentage of their daylight hours to meetings could manage this.[39]

Such a participatory way of dealing with public affairs seems fundamentally alien to a society such as ours where most people spend most of their daylight hours functioning in hierarchical organisations, carrying out the wishes of superiors. Not only is there a flagrant incongruity between the guiding philosophies of the two kind models, but the sheer demands on a person's time and attention would be too great to imagine the systems co-existing. Even it if were theoretically possible to accommodate both ways of life, free time now for most people in consumer-capitalist countries is split between activities that distract from work and those that induce rejuvenation in preparation for another spate of it. A society dominated by work and career aspirations is attuned— at best—to a representative political system, where the business of politics is (to use a modern term) outsourced to professionals whose jobs exist for precisely that purpose. The ancient Greeks would have named such a system

---

39  From David Graeber's foreword to Knapp, Flach, and Ayboga, *Revolution in Rojava*, xx.

oligarchy. Power is held by the few, not the many. Indeed, Aristotle asserted that both the development of virtue and "active participation in politics"—what his contemporaries called democracy—required leisure.

In the absence of economic or ecological collapse, it might seem that society is destined to remain trapped on the treadmill of work and consumption and politics condemned to remain the province of professionals and careerists. It is no fluke that the flare-ups of council democracy in recent times—the Rojavan revolution, the assemblies in Argentina and the indignados in Spain—all occurred in the wake of severe social crises, such as civil wars or economic downturns that made millions unemployed. The existing civil authorities were overwhelmed with what suddenly beset them—or in the Rojavan case simply upped and left after the uprising against the Assad regime—and the alternative institutions of democracy either stepped into the breach or attempted to play such a role. The disruption of the normal state of affairs—extreme in the case of Rojava—freed people from their day-to-day responsibilities and granted them the free time to participate in self-managing institutions. When such a vacuum does not arise, possibly the best that can be hoped for is that unwelcome interlopers—such as Jeremy Corbyn in the UK—disrupt the normal functioning of the system and restore a modicum of decency to the way it treats a growing number of people deemed superfluous to its accumulative needs.

However, if we relinquish for a moment the notion of revolution as a sudden eruption which instantaneously changes the course of society, then perhaps what Euro-

American societies are experiencing is a slow revolution. The 1990s and early 2000s were a profoundly subdued period politically in which the idea of liberal capitalism as the endpoint of history gained widespread credence. And if liberal capitalism was history's natural and inevitable destiny, its signature institutions—the multi-national corporation and representative, consensual government—were the outcome of a long moral evolution which had dethroned various forms of forced labour and authoritarian government, uncaging the natural inclinations of the individual to consume, exchange and amass wealth. However, since the 2008 crash, the temper of the times has changed immeasurably. This can be observed in outward signs—a "far-left" outsider on the verge of becoming British Prime Minister and a person who self-identifies as a socialist nearly becoming the Democratic nominee for President in the US (in addition to "socialist" Democrats, such as Alexandria Ocasio-Cortez, being elected Congress).[40] If you had suggested these scenarios to a political observer at the turn of the century, s/he would have regarded them as quite outlandish. There is obviously a sinister dimension to this historical turn—the far right is in power in several European countries, strong globally in far more, and Donald Trump occupies the White House. Liberal capitalism can be superseded by worse political and social systems as

40  To be clear Jeremy Corbyn's policies are social democratic rather than "far left" but, judged in terms of the rightward shift in British politics' centre of gravity since the beginning of the 1980s, he is an extremist. See Mat Little, "Jeremy Corbyn is not particularly left-wing," *We are not the Beautiful Blog*, July 2016.

well as by something better. But the unrivalled ascendancy of the market order, intellectually at least, is over.

What has been going on beneath the surface is a questioning of structures and institutions thought immutable and the rightful culmination of an ages old struggle for freedom. On the liberal side of the status quo it is axiomatic that this struggle is unfinished—that governing bodies and corporations need to be remoulded to accommodate the lives and demands of women, LGBT people and ethnic minorities. However, the questioning goes far deeper—the nature of the institutions and their claims to legitimacy is at stake, not merely how open and meritocratic they are. The common sense behind such questioning is now pervasive. For example, the idea that governments in Euro-American societies are oligarchies, rather than democracies, primarily representing their backers in the corporate sector and the rich rather than the broad swathe of voters is no longer a niche or extreme viewpoint. The finding of a 2014 Princeton university study that corporations, together with those at the summit of the income distribution, have a "substantial" influence over US government policy, in contrast to that of the average citizen, which is close to zero, may contradict, according to one of its authors, "decades of political science research."[41] But, to many, its conclusions were simply

---

41  See Martin Gilens and Benjamin I. Page, "Testing theories of American politics: Elites, interest groups and average citizens," Perspectives on Politics, September 2014; and Sahil Kapuir, "Scholar Behind Viral 'Oligarchy' Study Tells You What It Means," Talking Points Memo, 22 April 2014.

confirmation of glaring developments. The fact that politics and the media have become increasingly become closed, dynastic arenas, inaccessible to the vast majority of people, has also not gone unnoticed. If all revolutions are ultimately revolutions of contempt for those in power, as the French poet and politician Alphonse de Lamartine said of the 1848 revolution in France, then we are in a pre-revolutionary situation. Stanley Milgram likened obedience to sleep. For long periods, he said, we can be so thoroughly immersed in our social roles that, like a person in a deep sleep, we cannot be disturbed. But at other times, the obedient person is lightly dozing and can be awoken. Then the social order's contingent character, deliberately misconstrued by the powerful as fixed and immutable, becomes readily apparent.

In such a fluid and unpredictable situation, public policy can play contrasting roles. For example, calls for the introduction of a basic income (UBI)—an unconditional sum paid regularly to each person in contrast to means-tested and conditional welfare—could be used, as some right-wing libertarians advocate, to bolster people's willingness to accept low paid, temporary and irregular work, providing "continuous income for discontinuous work."[42] That is why supporters include Silicon Valley billionaires and business celebrities like Richard Branson. In many of the pilots that have begun recently, UBI has been framed in exactly that fashion, its success hinging on how effectively it incentivises work. The conservative effects of a basic income set at an

---

42 André Gorz, *Reclaiming Work: Beyond the Wage-Based Society* (Polity Press, 1999), 82.

"insufficient" level were predicted by the French thinker, André Gorz, two decades ago. "The lower the basic income, the greater will be the 'encouragement' to take any work at all," he said in 1997, "and the more new 'slavers' will be able to specialise in employing a cheap workforce in fly-by-night operations providing service work on a contract and subcontract basis."[43]

However, in other circumstances, and set at a "sufficient" level, UBI could have the opposite effect, acting to sever the link between income and work. It could represent a stepping-stone, allowing people to refuse or abandon work they didn't like and choose activities they wanted to devote attention to. This kind of UBI, thought Gorz, could break up the "work-based society" and allow one based on "multi-activity" to emerge. Each person from childhood onwards, he imagined, would be "involved in, and feel the attraction of, a general proliferation of artistic, sporting, techno-scientific, artisanal, political, philosophical, ecosophic, relational and cooperative activities all around him/her; a society in which means of production and facilities for self-providing are accessible to everyone at any time of day."[44] A UBI conceived in this way fulfils the conditions of post-scarcity, granting more free time whilst ensuring material security and enabling the skeleton of a participatory political system to be laid down. As one Swiss UBI campaigner said in advance of that country's referendum on the issue in 2014, basic income "sets human forces free in ways one may never have thought about."[45]

---

43  Ibid., 81.

44  Ibid., 91.

45  Marilola Wili, in an interview with members of Generation Basic

*Unconditional* basic income could, in fact, be seen as an evocation of humanity's non-obedient past. There are unmistakable similarities between UBI and the "irreducible minimum"—the "inalienable right" to food, shelter and clothing irrespective of work contributed that Bookchin believed marked tribal societies before the emergence of civilisation. That prehistoric humanity was probably not as uniformly egalitarian as he and other radical anthropologists have suggested does not detract from the centrality of interdependence and care for others to early human bands. That pristine ethos, directed only towards other members of the group—maybe just three dozen people commonly—must be universalised.

The effects of a sufficient basic income on actually existing capitalism are difficult to predict. One possible consequence is that, in complete contrast to minimal basic income, the heavy emphasis currently placed on the exploitation of cheap labour becomes unsustainable. As argued in Chapter 3, despite dire predictions of epoch-making technological upheaval, modern-day capitalism seems peculiarly ineffectual at actually delivering such a transformation. Aided by in-work state benefits, it has chosen model of exploitation that eschews major investment in new technologies in favour of unimaginative use of readily accessible human labour. A sufficient UBI might encourage automation to take place by virtue of the fact that legions of value adding human labourers are no longer available.

---

Income, "We're facing a shift in what work means and it is this generation that can express this shift," *We are not the Beautiful*, 23 October, 2013.

However, contemporary financialised capitalism is also immensely precarious. The 2008 economic crash was arrested by huge government intervention, record low interest rates and the creation of artificial asset booms through massive increases in the money supply. This stopped the bust wreaking Great Depression-style havoc but at the cost of increasing the level of debt in the economy. Debt, especially corporate debt, is enormous.[46] Another recession—which in the history of capitalism always happens periodically—could set off a chain reaction of debt default, producing the bankruptcy of all kinds of institutions, including pension funds. In such circumstances, amidst dwindling government tax revenue, it might seem that the introduction of any kind of UBI will inevitably be forestalled.

However, the reaction of governments—and pan-government bodies like the EU and IMF—to a renewed downturn is almost certainly going to entail more severe austerity, coupled with money creation and even negative interest rates. The tolerance of society for the first is by now wearing thin and an alternative response, empowered by public revulsion for neoliberalism, may well gain ground. This will involve public ownership and control of financial institutions and, very possibly, the establishment of a basic income funded by what Gorz called the "pooling of socially

---

46  According to one ratings agency, between 2011 and 2017, global non-financial corporate debt grew by 15 percentage points to 96% of world GDP: https://www.bloomberg.com/news/articles/2018-02-05/s-p-warns-high-corporate-debt-could-trigger-next-default-cycle

produced wealth," if for no other reason than the utilitarian ambition that public spending power is maintained.

Whatever the precise circumstances, in a post-crash world, a debilitated, politically discredited, capitalist sector will prove even less able to expedite major technological advancements. However, in order to become reality post-scarcity requires an agent to bring it into being. Who that agent of technological transformation will be—whether the role is assumed by municipalities, central government or the cooperative sector—is at present hard to predict. Jonathan Korsár argues that "new social organizations" are needed to facilitate and deal with the ramifications of new technologies.[47] He suggests that municipalities are uniquely placed to fill the gap, in part because the once the start-up costs of new technologies, such as the harvesting of renewable energy, are settled, the operating costs are minimal. The lure of profit, unless artificially inserted into the process, is unlikely to be the prime motivation.

However, just as a post-scarcity society requires "new social organizations" economically, it summons them politically. The past is always seen through the prism of the present. In this sense, Arendt's 19th and 20th century revolutionary councils, much like the communes of Rojava,

---

47 "We need new systems of interaction between new technologies, and new social organizations that can meet and manage the demands of increased productivity from these new technologies." Jonathan Korsár, "Toward a Zero Marginal Cost Municipality," in Eirik Eiglad, ed., *Social Ecology and Social Change* (New Compass, 2015), 144-152.

are invariably dismissed—should they even be considered—as freakish accidents signifying nothing. Arendt herself saw them as the "lost treasure" of the revolutionary tradition. In the future, they may well be seen in quite a different light—as harbingers of a social order whose time had not yet come.

## The Disobedient Society

In Stanley Milgram's obedience experiments it wasn't the obedient who paid the "physic cost." It wasn't that those who obeyed the experimenter's orders to inflict what they believed were possibly lethal electric shocks weren't troubled by what they were instructed to do. During the experiment they sweated, laughed hysterically or dug their fingernails into their skin. But ultimately, obedience supplied a kind of contentment, the satisfaction of having done the right thing. "It is compliance that carries the positive connotation," observed Milgram.[48] The disobedient, by contrast, were plagued by anxiety and a gnawing sense of faithlessness. They had "disrupted the social order" and it was they, rather than the obedient subjects, who were burdened by their actions.[49]

To Milgram, the difficulty of disobedience meant that the pressure to be obedient—to be voluntarily transformed into an instrument for carrying out the wishes of another—had to be deeply embedded within the psyche. It was a kind of reflex action which transcended time or place. In fact, Milgram concluded, in an echo of Charles Darwin, that humans had

---

48  Milgram, Obedience to Authority, 165.

49  Ibid.

evolved to be obedient. When autonomous humans come together in organisations, they don't assess orders from above in terms of personal standards of morality, but simply carry them out. This willingness to merge into the collective was how Homo sapiens, initially only one species of hominin among at least five others, survived and prospered, driving its rivals to extinction.

An alternative to Milgram's explanation does not rest on the superficiality of obedience. It is, indeed, deeply embedded in the psyche. But deeply embedded does not mean innate. Over millennia of rule of humans over other humans, obedience—a theoretically autonomous individual acting as an agent for a person of higher status—became implanted as natural and divinely ordained. The slave obeyed the owner, the serf obeyed the lord, the wife obeyed the husband and the worker obeyed the employer. In societies of inescapable scarcity, this repressive psychological sensibility was fortified by the awareness of rulers that their freedom was inextricably linked to the domination of others. Without obedience for most, freedom for some would perish. We are all the heirs of this legacy, materially and mentally.

However, we are now at the stage in history when this zero sum game no longer applies. Freedom can be universalised. This potentially means the end of obedience, which now primarily takes the form of ubiquitous wage labour. Among future generations mass wage labour, as Jeremy Rifkin asserts, may well come to be viewed with the same sense of disbelief that we look upon chattel slavery and serfdom now.

A disobedient society does not imply the end of discipline, cooperation or episodic sovereignty. It is still a society. But it will mean that authority needs to justify itself at all times—in a society shorn of obedience people will not allow themselves to be transformed into unthinking agents for the desires of order-givers. Just as important, the fear that they will be forced to play such a role will be gone.

To the degree that a "sphere of necessity" still exists, labour (the satisfaction of repetitive, insistent needs as Arendt defined it) will have to be carried out. However, the organisations that execute these tasks will be governed by a rotation of functions ("to be ruled and ruled in turn," as the Greeks put it) so that a permanent separation doesn't develop between workers and overseers, order-takers and order-givers. The activity of work will not be accompanied by the "alteration of attitude" that Milgram deemed an essential part of obedience.[50] The traditional objection that in a society where nobody is subject to the pressure of material need, unpleasant work would just go undone, is met by the contention that in a society dedicated to resolving the problem of the powerlessness of the individual, distasteful, arduous labour will lose much of its baleful aura. Besides, no-one will be fatally fixed in the condition of endless wage labour and automation will gradually reduce the need for human labour.[51]

The political system appropriate to this coordination of individual desires is not a representative one in which consent is extracted by professional politicians. It is a

---

50  Milgram, *Obedience to Authority*, 135.

51  The one area where automation is not appropriate is caring labour, particularly of the elderly.

different—some would say genuine—form of democracy in which opinions and policies are first formed at a base level and then transmitted upwards by delegates who can always be recalled if they don't embody the desires of the base. In order for this democratic *society* to function—and to avoid its degeneration into a devitalised shell controlled by professional politicians and activists—generalised free time is required. The continuance of time-devouring mass wage labour all but guarantees its failure and the return of obedience and rule by elites.

However, a disobedient society can still be a conformist one. This represents its hidden danger, in my opinion. Obedience is different from conformity. An obedient person carries out the orders of superiors without imitating the behaviour of the order-giver. A conformist person mirrors the speech, beliefs and acts of associates. Conformity, as Milgram observed, leads to "homogenisation of behaviour" and can occur in a society without any tangible grading between members. It is, to misuse a current phrase, a "peer-to-peer" phenomenon.

Hannah Arendt believed that conformism was inherent in society. Such conformism was acute in what she termed "mass society"—the atomized collection of individuals that the modern, market economy has produced who are defined by imitative behaviour and uniform taste. Such individuals—dubbed "job holders" by Arendt—identify themselves with their careers, are concerned solely with their private interests and have a studied indifference towards others who are persecuted by society. A popular democracy founded on this basis, it might be imagined, would merely amplify desires and opinions that had already been granted the seal of approval, so to speak. It would be democratic in form but not in content. In a sense, though, this is a baseless fear—the mere act of creating a face-to-face democracy would transform the mass into a public where, in C. Wright Mill's phrase, "virtually as many people express opinions as receive them." However, this public, despite its apparent multiplicity of viewpoints, could still be conformist.

What makes conformity especially corrosive of free thinking is the tendency of those in its grip to deny that it is happening, to assert their independence of mind. Thus, the silent moral pressure it exerts—to agree despite inner misgivings, or to fail to voice alternative points of view—can occur in an atmosphere of apparent plurality, tolerance and receptivity. All revolutions, all political movements implicitly resent transgressions against their interpretation of reality and their version of common sense. This tendency runs deep in a revolutionary tradition seared by the experience that any radical divergence from the status quo is instantly surrounded by enemies intent on its destruction. Thus, the dominant group, the majority could insist on the legitimacy and primacy of its view of the world without the imposition of any kind of coercion. But if democracy ever becomes the purpose of society, rather than just a means to a predetermined end, then the impulse to cultivate uniformity must be resisted. In fact, the opposite—dissent—must be encouraged.

Bookchin's concept of dissensus has, in my opinion, a centrality to a future society which has not been fully appreciated. Dissensus means that opinions that diverge from the consensus of the majority are not merely tolerated but actively encouraged. After a decision has been reached on any issue, the dissenting minority has the right to continue their dissent, to articulate reasoned arguments as why it should be overturned. Even if their position is unpopular, they should not conform to the view of the majority unless rationally convinced. In part, this obduracy stems from a recognition that, throughout history, important ideas that have become accepted as common sense have started as the claims of minorities, even tiny minorities. Dissensus is the acknowledgement that, while accession to majority opinion is necessary for democracy to function, that judgement is not infallible and quite often wrong.

But dissensus is much more than the awareness that minority opinion should be cultivated because of its eventual usefulness and wisdom. It also follows from the belief that democracy and politics are not mere instruments to achieve a desired goal; they have a purpose in their own right and are essential components of a mix of activities that are part of being fully human. They are, to go back to Arendt, an integral part of a lost revolutionary tradition. Discussion, forming opinions and changing your mind are essential to the *practice* of democracy and politics. Dissent is creative and "valuable in itself as an ongoing democratic phenomenon."[52] Without dissensus, disobedience can easily morph into acquiescence with the transitory opinions and morality of the majority; it can become a tributary flowing into Rousseau's undivided general will. This is not liberation but a "nightmare world

---

52  From Murray Bookchin, *Anarchism, Marxism and the Future of the Left* (AK Press, 1999), 149.

of intellectual and psychic conformity."[53] "Freedom", as Rosa Luxemburg famously said, "is always and exclusively for the one who thinks differently."[54]

One hundred years ago, on 23 March 1919, around 100 people, an assortment of black-shirted army veterans, futurists, nationalists and syndicalists, attended the inaugural meeting of what would become the Italian Fascist party. The hall in Milan where the first *fascio di combattimento* met was provided by local businessmen. And despite an initial flirtation with left-wing ideas and economic democracy, the movement's slogan—*obedience, not discussion*—presciently described how it would evolve.[55] Fascism became an attempt to extend the obedience enacted by economic institutions—corporations and landowners—into the political realm. Decisions flowed downwards from a supreme leader to be obeyed by subordinates. That is why Fascism's economic doctrine was given the name corporatism, Noam Chomsky described corporations as "in political terms, fascist," and why Fascism was inherently totalitarian.

---

53  Ibid.

54  A worrying tendency of the modern Left is the refusal to debate with people it disagrees with. So-called "no platforming" has outgrown its original—and justifiable—purpose of denying the oxygen of publicity to outright Fascists into an unwillingness to argue publicly with a range of dissenting opinions, even opinions within the same political parties and broad currents. This does not bode well for how a multiplicity of opinions would be dealt with in popular assemblies.

55  Harrison, *The Rebellious Suffragette*, 284.

Being anti-fascist is more than combatting resurgent Fascism. It is about reversing its core belief system. "Discussion, not obedience" should be the rallying cry a movement intent on breathing democracy into the political realm and into spheres previously thought the exclusive domain of authority and submission. This ambition, which appeared thoroughly utopian in previous ages, is now a practical possibility because, materially, history's realm of freedom is now potentially open to everybody. Such a step forward in human existence might still seem unlikely. According to Hannah Arendt, every new beginning that breaks into the world wears the garb of an "infinite improbability."[56] But historical processes are both created and interrupted by human initiative, by the fact that humanity ultimately creates its own reality. Expecting the unexpected is merely being realistic.

---

56  From "What is Freedom?" in *The Portable Hannah Arendt*, 459.